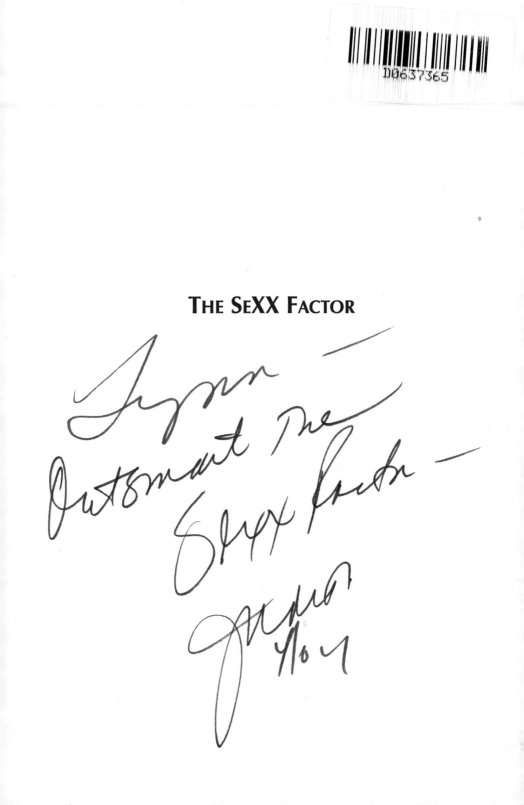

THE SeXX FACTOR

THE SeXX FACTOR

Breaking the Unwritten Codes
that Sabotage Personal and Professional Lives

Marilou Ryder, Ed.D.
and
Judith Briles, Ph.D.

New Horizon Press
Far Hills, New Jersey

New Horizon Press
P.O. Box 669
Far Hills, NJ 07931

Marilou Ryder and Judith Briles
    The SeXX Factor: Breaking the Unwritten Codes that Sabotage Personal
    and Professional Lives

Cover Design: Robert Aulicino
Interior Design: Susan M. Sanderson

Library of Congress Control Number: 2002102378

ISBN: 0-88282-218-7
New Horizon Press

Manufactured in the U.S.A.

2007   2006   2005   2004   2003   /   5   4   3   2   1

Dedication Page

To all the women in the world who desire, deserve and have earned a place in the world of power.

Authors' Note

This book is based on extensive personal interviews of women and men involved in a variety of business, professional, educational, religious, social and charitable organizations, associations and workplaces as well as research in the areas of sociology, psychology and gender issues. The names and identifying characteristics of some people in this book have been changed in order to protect privacy.

Table of Contents

Acknowledgements

From Marilou...
I would like to express my heartfelt appreciation to the many individuals who shared their stories of personal and business successes and problems with me over the past ten years. I have talked to so many people in many different arenas, it is impossible to mention them all by name. While the majority of the men and women interviewed chose to remain anonymous, I am deeply impressed and indebted by their generosity of spirit in entrusting me with their stories and deepest concerns about women's communication with men in all areas of life as well as women's access to positions of power.

From Judith...
For twenty plus years, women and men have freely shared with me their stories of workplace dilemmas and gender dissonance—they number in the thousands. So many times, it would have been easy to put my listening on automatic, as one story overlapped the next and too many blended with another. Thankfully, I didn't. Although many are alike, none are the same.

The Women's Movement was birthed before my two daughters were born. As adults, they assume that where they are today is a normal function of doing well and being rewarded via recognition, promotions and money. Yet, they've run into their share of stone walls...and then they remember—the elevator to success makes plenty of stops along the way. Some of the stops seem out of place, stupid and/or unreasonable. Then they are reminded that there are plenty of people within a power base to judge them, to block them along their journey.

No one creates a book solo. It takes the efforts of many people to deliver ideas, thoughts and observations. Joan Dunphy continues to publish books that make a difference; co-author Marilou Ryder created a wonderful new phrase—*The SeXX Factor*—that illustrates how women differ from men in their behaviors and prejudices creating dissonance in their family and professional lives; and Barbara Munson is the perfect person to bounce ideas off and editor extraordinaire.

Preface

The SeXX Factor—it's a catchy title, but what is it? What do we mean by the SeXX Factor and how does it apply to you and other women and men? How can it—how will it—impact your life? Let's start by understanding what we mean by the SeXX Factor.

This is our definition of the SeXX Factor:

The SeXX Factor—
Behaviors, attitudes and strategies of women that inhibit, encumber or impede their interactions with men in their personal and professional lives. These behaviors produce a subconscious discomfort or uneasiness in men, who react by getting angry, confused or resentful. Women end up dealing with unnecessary roadblocks and traps in their personal, family and business domains.

We bring decades of experience to writing *The SeXX Factor*. Since the mid-eighties, both of us have researched and spoken to thousands of women and men about their personal and professional lives. Each of us conducted multiple studies—some with a respondent sample of one hundred and others with over five thousand. Collectively, we've heard many women speak...sometimes softly, sometimes with fierce intensity.

Marilou has spent most of her adult life in academe. The resulting understanding and expertise has created for her a broad and defining view of the leadership roles in the education field. A developing passion for women's issues drove her to discover a new way to think about the interaction of men and women in the workplace. Throughout her studies, she asked these two leading questions,

Why is it that women do not have/cannot gain equal access to the top positions in business and education or to positions of power in life?

Why is it that women who are as smart and work as hard as men still continue to lose out in attaining top positions at work?

Marilou enrolled in the graduate department of California State University of Long Beach in 1988 and began her first official study of women in leadership positions. While the ultimate goal was to receive an educational administrative credential, her studies culminated in a research position paper entitled "Women in Educational Leadership." Her research clearly indicated that women were not gaining access to high-level positions in their organizations.

One of her studies surveyed one hundred female school administrators in California. A positive result there suggested that women were beginning to break through internal and external barriers that once prevented them from attaining positions as principals, coordinators and assistant superintendents. Her findings, summarized in the paper entitled, "Women in Educational Administration: Breaking the Statistical Norm," were published in *Thrust for Educational Leadership* (1994), an important educational journal for public school administrators.

Marilou continued to read and analyze current literature that related to women's advancement in educational leadership. She noted that women were gaining parity with men in all educational leadership positions (principals, coordinators, directors and assistant superintendents) with one astonishing exception, the top position. There were few women superintendents! Was there something that she wasn't aware of that prevented women from gaining positions of power? She was determined to find out...

Judith worked in investments in the sixties and seventies, first, as a broker's assistant, then as a top producing stockbroker with E.F. Hutton in 1972. She approached her superiors multiple times about moving into a management position. Repeatedly, she was rebuffed. There were no women in management and no plans to include any. Frustrated, a few years later, she said goodbye to Corporate America. Upon resigning, she started her own firm specializing in financial planning for women. In 1986, she sold the company and transitioned to being a full-time professional speaker, writer and researcher with an emphasis on workplace issues. Since then, she has created, implemented and published dozens of research projects that concentrated on workplace issues. Judith has spoken in every state plus ten countries on topics concerning women—specifically, sabotage in the workplace, confidence and personal finance.

After completing a Masters in Business Administration, she later returned to complete a Doctorate in Business Administration. During this time, she noticed a phenomenon among working women—many claimed to be supportive of other women, yet in practice, didn't walk their talk. Her doctoral dissertation probed the issue of women, ethics and sabotage in the workplace and was based on a nationwide study of two thousand men and women. Throughout her studies, she continuously asked,

Do women usually support other women?

Do women undermine or withdraw their support of
*   other women?*

And if they do, why?

Is sisterhood a myth?

Is there a gender difference when it comes to workplace
*   sabotage and bullying?*

Do women handle confrontations differently than men?

The results of her work were published in 1987 in *Woman to Woman: From Sabotage to Support.* Identified as a pioneering work in the area of women's workplace relationships, she has conducted five additional in-depth studies that include in excess of 10,000 respondents. Subsequent published works on the topic include *The Briles Report on Women in Healthcare, GenderTraps, Woman to Woman 2000* and *Zapping Conflict in the Health Care Workplace.*

The SeXX Factor and Gender Dissonance
Marilou returned to school in the mid-nineties as a doctoral candidate in Leadership and Management. She formulated the hypothesis that the SeXX Factor (which she also termed gender dissonance) was an important factor preventing women's advancement in private and professional domains. It became the subject of her thesis. She identified four areas as primary foci within the study of behaviors that women were reported to use or display: role confusion, communication differences, cultural differences and women's personal power issues.

Completing her research, Marilou determined that the SeXX Factor was indeed an important component that prevented women from gaining access to positions of power. It was time to expand her research to the corporate workplace. In numerous interviews, successful men and women confirmed that many of the behaviors caused men to experience the phenomenon identified as the SeXX Factor.

The majority of these corporate men and women also concluded that these behaviors served as a barrier for women wanting equal access to positions of power in their organizations.

Judith, meanwhile, was also probing what would be called gender dissonance or static among women and found that it too could be a deterrent to women moving ahead and up. Like Marilou, Judith probed and published studies concerning role confusion, gender disparities, communication differences, cultural differences, confrontational methods and styles and overall power issues. Some of the behaviors and actions could be identified as intentional, others unintentional. Styles used could be overtly or covertly delivered. And, there were distinct differences in gender dominated workplaces. Judith identified them as *Sabotage Factors*, behaviors and actions of others that eroded reputations, destroyed self-esteem and confidence and ruined careers.

The SeXX Factor Behaviors

Initially, sixty-four behaviors/situations were identified from the first study by Marilou. Since, then, additional behaviors have been identified by the authors—bringing the total to more than one hundred—that men report are triggers for them. Some seem minor and silly to women, from wearing too much jewelry or frilly clothing, sharing feelings or gossiping, to threatening sexual harassment, challenging a man on his inappropriate behavior (whether one-on-one or in front of others) or acting too assertively or aggressively.

It wasn't uncommon for women, when learning of the SeXX Factor, to be surprised that men would avoid them if they were too crude or they cursed—*What do you mean? If I curse in front of them, men are put off?* Other women were stunned when they discovered that behaviors such as refusing to accept traditional courtesies from men, talking too much or working long hours into the night might cause men to feel angry and resentful.

The SeXX Factor revisits both these women's theses and introduces a new one similar to that of Daniel Goldman's *Emotional Intelligence* and Gail Sheehy's *The Silent Passage*. Where Goldman clarified the work of Eileen Rockefeller Growald in that people have an Emotional IQ, and Sheehy unveils women's stages of life, *The SeXX Factor* reveals how and why too many women are diverted from the upper echelons of business and positions of leadership in their endeavors outside the workplace and gives solutions to avoid future road blocks. Understanding the analysis of *The SeXX Factor* means that any woman will have the keys to open doors to positions of power!

Introduction

For stay-at-home moms who must interact with their children's male sports coaches to teachers to female executives who've had their heads bruised on the proverbial glass ceiling, here is the ultimate guide to smooth interaction instead of friction between the sexes. We wrote this book to provide women who must deal with men and men who must deal with women in their professional and private lives the key to understanding each other.

This book focuses on four areas: (1) Role Confusion; (2) Communication Differences; (3) Cultural Differences; (4) Women's and Men's Power Issues. Here we identify one hundred specific behaviors that cause women the most trouble and men the most anger and confusion when they deal with each other. We disclose the emotional and cyclical ways that the SeXX Factor prevents women from succeeding, men from attaining real understanding and both sexes from meeting on an equal playing field.

We hope that this book's revelations will decode negative behaviors and antiquated patterns for both sexes and will open the doors of communication, permitting equality of power in both men's and women's personal and professional lives.

The SeXX Factor will appeal to women of all ages and lifestyles (and men who want to understand them) who want to move forward—be it in their careers or personal lives. For instance:

- Women on their way up the career ladder will want to know how the *SeXX Factor* can result in a *power quotient.* Upwardly mobile career women can use this information to plan for the future.

- "Stay-at-home moms" who confront the SeXX Factor on a daily basis will learn from this book how to deal more successfully with male stock brokers and financial consultants, physicians, sports coaches and soccer dads.

- Women entrenched in their careers can extend their knowledge and use the results obtained from taking the quizzes in this book to provide additional keys to open upper-level organizational doors.

- Women in positions close to the top level will be able to strategize the final steps needed to access the upper organizational stairways leading to top positions of power.

- Career counselors, career consultants and psychologists can study the behaviors outlined in *The SeXX Factor* and share them as awareness indicators for women who are facing friction in their male/female interactions.

- Women of all ages will gain a greater insight with regard to working and living with powerful men in their personal and professional lives. Using the clear-cut strategies delineated, they will finally begin to clearly communicate on power issues and gain and utilize power while interacting with their husbands and other men in their lives: physicians, car mechanics, managers, supervisors as well as their children's school and sports personnel.

- Men who desire to keep up with current trends and further their understanding about power and gender issues will want to read this revealing account of how women can overcome the SeXX Factor and improve their personal and professional lives.

Why haven't we heard about the SeXX Factor in our personal lives and in the workplace? Probably because people (women in particular) have been blaming and using the glass ceiling and the battle between the sexes, among other things, as excuses for why they haven't been able to handle personal and professional interactions in which they must deal with men. It's convenient to blame somebody or something else, but it doesn't provide answers or solutions.

The SeXX Factor is about us, as women, and how we affect those men who are influential in our professional and private lives. Men in positions of power often feel uncomfortable when they interact with women who behave in certain ways. Men usually are unaware of what causes the SeXX Factor. They are aware, however, that they don't like how they feel and thus want to avoid feeling that way at all costs. What this means for women is that, in order to avoid the discomfort, men in power will prevent women from functioning well in their world.

Why should we care about men's discomfort with women's behavior?
We must care, because men's discomfort with certain female behaviors is affecting our lives both privately and publicly. While it may seem that women are making great strides in the world, statistics indicate that it will likely take women another one hundred years to achieve equal parity with men in many areas.

Why should we change our behavior for the sake of men? We aren't changing for the sake of men…it's for our own sake! Men have always done whatever it takes to get power. Women must now do so as well. Women already at the top know that men in power continually do what it takes…they are in control…they are determined…they don't complain when something doesn't go right or blame it on being a "man." They've got all the right moves and they recognize what's required to achieve power.

Successful women understand this same principle and know what they've had to do to obtain and keep their own power. They have also become aware that some of their behaviors cause problems for men. They know that it exists and are mindful of its effects on men. They know that if they confuse, frustrate or annoy men who hold power over them, they lose out on chances to achieve their goals, whether these be in their family lives or business lives. A woman's awareness of the SeXX Factor allows her to even the playing field so she can achieve the success she deserves.

Still don't get it? You may think that if men feel annoyed or uncomfortable when women act in a certain way—like using profanity or gossiping—that's their problem, not women's. But it is women's problem—it's the enemy within, so to speak. Our behaviors and habits, many of which are linked to historical female styles of behavior, often cause men to experience the SeXX Factor. The identification and correction of behaviors that cause this is an important ingredient in helping us gain power at work and in our everyday lives.

Learning from the past and altering those behaviors that cause men to experience the SeXX Factor are not about trying to make men feel better. It's about following some basic principles that will help women gain new habits, behaviors and attitudes to change how men view women in terms of power and competency.

The basic principles to help you gain access to working more successfully with men are simple. First, come to grips with the fact that some behaviors or habits cause men to experience the SeXX Factor. Second, change those behaviors or habits.

This book shatters currently held notions about why women often fail to successfully interact in a powerful manner both personally and professionally. It will give you practical strategies to help you rise above gender politics and get on your path to success, fully handling conflicts that are holding you back and causing friction when dealing with male authority figures. No longer will you be stymied by the conflict between the sexes.

Who knows what women can be when they are finally free to become themselves?

The Feminine Mystique
Betty Friedan, 1962

Who knows what women can be when they finally understand themselves?

The SeXX Factor
Marilou Ryder and Judith Briles, 2003

1

The SeXX Factor:
Doing What Comes Naturally?

No book or work about women and their behaviors and mannerisms can be created without looking in the mirror and studying ourselves, but we also need to go further than that—we must look *through* the mirror and examine how men view what women do. Do they regard women's behaviors differently from their own behaviors? Are they more tolerant of idiosyncrasies and mannerisms generated by other men than by women? Do men have any idea of behaviors or mannerisms that they do or use that works against them? Whether men are self-aware or not is the subject of another book, not this one. What we are going to look into here are the things women do in both their personal and professional lives that cause them difficulties in succeeding within a power culture that is still predominantly comprised of men.

Driving Him Crazy

Men interviewed across the country have reported there are some things that women do in the home, workplace, school or social venues that drive them crazy. Most of these behaviors are not hugely annoying or disruptive—they're more like buzzing gnats than biting horseflies. But, over a period of time, they can become major triggers and button pushers. As one male executive confessed, "They add up."

These triggers include:

- Gossiping
- Refusing to allow a man to open a door for them
- Refusing to allow a man to pull out a chair for them
- Swearing or using crude language
- Clarifying their thoughts by thinking out loud
- Wearing excessively ruffled or frilly clothing, blouses or dresses or being over-laden with jewelry
- Challenging a man's expertise in public
- Putting a hand on a man's knee or touching him (this assumes there is not a romantic involvement)
- Saying "I'm sorry" repeatedly, offering apologies, using hedging or tag types of questions
- Using sarcasm to prove a point
- Saying "I" rather than "We" in conversations
- Talking too much about nothing
- Crying
- Bringing up issues that have already been discussed, addressed and dealt with

Truth be told—men are put off when they encounter women who exhibit these types of female behaviors and actions. And there's more! At last count, powerful men and women already at the top have identified a minimum of one hundred different behaviors that men say make them uncomfortable. When this happens, the SeXX Factor surfaces—it's men's reaction to women who display any of these behaviors.

The SeXX Factor?
Simply put, the SeXX Factor, which we also call "power static" or "gender dissonance," is a term that was developed after years of research and supporting interviews conducted with thousands of powerful men and women in top positions in government, law, business and education. Successful men disclosed that they have witnessed other men feeling uneasy or unsettled when they interacted with powerful women. They also revealed that they have experienced these same feelings when they relate to women at work or in other environments. *Moreover, they disclosed that when men feel unsettled*

or confused about a woman and her behavior (whether actual or perceived), the result is that she is usually blocked from top power positions or achieving the success or goals she desires.

Want to know more? For starters, let's look at the definition again.

The SeXX Factor:
Behaviors, attitudes and strategies of women that inhibit, encumber or impede them within and outside the workplace. These behaviors produce a subconscious discomfort or uneasiness in men, who react by getting angry, confused or resentful. Women end up dealing with unnecessary roadblocks and traps in both their personal and professional lives.

Now, are you ready for the challenge? Take the following quiz to help you identify behaviors that cause men to experience the SeXX Factor. You may discover, for example, that talking too much in staff meetings or school conferences may cause some men to experience frustration and anger. You can then use this powerful knowledge and corresponding practical solutions to overcome your need to "over-talk," better positioning yourself in your private and professional domains. You can determine the results of your personal assessment and come up with your own Power Static Quotient. Are you ready?

Take the SeXX Factor Quiz
Read through the entire list and score each item on the appropriate blank line that most closely describes your current behavior when you interact with males in your private life or on the job. Ask another person who you consider to be a critical, yet non-judgmental friend or colleague to check each item in the appropriate space that he believes most closely describes your behavior in your personal and work life when dealing with men. It is preferable to have a male friend or colleague answer these questions. Ask him to be honest and candid. Compare his answers to yours. Don't be surprised if you have opposing points of view.

Answer *Yes, No* or *Not Sure* to the following:

Do men ever perceive that you...	You			Critical Friend or Colleague		
	Yes	No	Not Sure	Yes	No	Not Sure
1. Use a "snippy" tone of voice when you disagree with men?	___	___	___	___	___	___
2. Refuse to accept "traditional" courtesies from men (i.e. opening of doors)?	___	___	___	___	___	___
3. Challenge men's expertise in public?	___	___	___	___	___	___
4. Talk or gossip too much?	___	___	___	___	___	___
5. Act overly assertive or confident causing men to refer to you as "tough to work with?"	___	___	___	___	___	___
6. Wear professional attire that is overly female or frilly?	___	___	___	___	___	___
7. Consistently work longer hours than the men?	___	___	___	___	___	___
8. Habitually say, "I'm sorry" or offer apologies when you speak or are late?	___	___	___	___	___	___
9. Consistently ask others for their opinions before making decisions?	___	___	___	___	___	___
10. Use collaboration or shared decision making that men feel takes up too much time?	___	___	___	___	___	___
11. Act "catty" when talking about women you don't like?	___	___	___	___	___	___
TOTAL:	___			___		

Scoring—Total the number of checks in each "Yes" column. Note the differences in your scores versus the scores your friend/colleague gave you. If "Not Sure" was marked, the response is usually a "Yes."

8-11 You're in Big Trouble
When men relate to you in personal and business settings, they continuously experience emotions and feelings related to The SeXX Factor. Review the entire list and circle those areas that you believe would be valuable for you to monitor and create a plan to modify, change and eliminate self-sabotaging behaviors.

4-7 You Need a Jump-start
Not too bad on the SeXX Factor Meter! You are aware of the many differences between men and women and understand how some of your actions may cause men to experience The SeXX Factor. Circle 3 or 4 specific behaviors that you would like to target and create an action plan to become more aware of their impact on men and how to eliminate them.

0-3 You're on Your Way to the Top!
You are definitely aware of what it takes to be a woman in a man's world! You are aware that men often hold the power over important personal areas as well as business dealings such as who gets promoted. Now help a colleague or friend conquer the SeXX Factor.

A Trip Down Memory Lane...
Now that you know where you stand in terms of "power static" and "gender dissonance," be aware that both Judith and Marilou have personally experienced fallout from the SeXX Factor. So have millions of other women. Join them on their journey of ups and downs...

1952...Sandra Day O'Connor received her law degree from Stanford University, graduating within the top five of her class. Initially, no one would hire her—"she was just a girl." Wanting to use her newly earned degree, she had no choice—she was forced to become self-employed and started her own firm.

1959...Nancy DiMarco received her master's degree in landscape architecture from Syracuse University. Having received a full scholarship and graduated magna cum laude, she had high hopes of landing a position with a prestigious landscape architecture firm in her hometown. "They told me the work

might be too hard for a woman. 'Perhaps you'd like to be the office manager,'
they suggested."

1960...As a ten-year-old girl, Marilou asked her father if it would
be possible for her to become a member of one of the Little League
baseball teams in town. Playing baseball with her classmates after
school, she rarely ever missed the opportunity to hit the ball out of the
neighborhood stadium. Her batting average was better than most of
the boys. Her father was president of the Optimist Club and promised
that he would ask his fellow club members if she could join one of the
Little League teams they sponsored. Since he had five daughters, she
thought that he took her request seriously. Marilou didn't know that
a ten-year-old girl had little to no chance to play on a boys' baseball
team.

1962...As a teenager, Judith was active in her school—excelling
academically as well as being an officer on the student council and a
cheerleader. With her grades, she assumed that she would be supported in her desire to attend college and become a doctor. When she
brought the subject up to her parents, she was stonewalled. College
was for boys/men, she was told—Judith had three brothers. Any
money saved would be directed toward their educations, not hers. She
was encouraged to apply at the community college for nursing
school—after all, she would most likely marry and have kids, wasting
money that her brothers could use. At sixteen, Judith graduated from
high school and did the expected. She got married and had three kids
by the time she was twenty.

1966...Sally Hansen remembers her first encounter penetrating the upper
echelons of corporate America. "We were pioneers. We had to really prove our-
selves. We had no mentors, no role models and no real help to get to the top. We
were often perceived as 'odd' and 'troublemakers.' After getting married in 1973
and having my first child, I finally stayed home and followed my husband's
success."

1967...All through high school, Marilou wanted to be a hair-
dresser. She made money cutting or styling her girlfriends' hair for
weddings and proms. Her father had different ideas. Unlike Judith's
father, he declared that all five of his daughters would attend college.

He openly worried that some of them might not be able to land husbands capable of supporting them...so a college education was in
order, just in case. No beauty school for Marilou. After looking
through the college catalogs in the high school guidance office, a
stark realization took place. There were two distinct career options:
become a nurse or a teacher. Accepted into the School of Education
at Adelphi University in New York, she began her journey toward a
career as an elementary school teacher.

1969...With two kids in school and the third in pre-school, Judith
decided to revisit her dream of being a surgeon. Knowing that she
needed an undergraduate degree with an emphasis in science, she
enrolled at the local community college and enthusiastically attended
classes. Six months into classes, she made an appointment with the
dean of the medical school at the University of Southern California
seeking his advice on which courses to take. Her dreams were shot
down within minutes—he told her that she would most likely not complete her undergraduate degree; that she would probably end up
divorced and he wanted to know what she was doing to prevent
becoming pregnant again.

1969...*Gina Reynolds was one of the first female truck drivers in New
York State. "I was treated as a freak. I overheard the manager talking to one of
his employees, 'She must be one of those homosexuals or transvestites. Actually,
on second thought, I think she was sent here by the government to see if we'd
actually hire her. She won't last.'"*

1971...During Marilou's first year as a fifth grade teacher, she
proved her father wrong. She got married, thought seriously about
having a baby and began to do hairstyling on the side. Her husband,
a graduate student at Syracuse University, invited her to attend a lecture that was being given by the president of NOW, the National
Organization of Women. Her life changed that day. She became fasci-
nated with the topic of women and immediately began to study and
write about women's issues. "Why is it," she asked, "that so few career
options exist for women?"

1972...Judith was divorced and fired from her job as a broker's
assistant within the same year. Stunned, and knowing that she had

three kids to support, she began looking for work. Not knowing where to start, she tried secretarial positions. She had been told that the reason she was "let go" was because she was going through a divorce and management felt she wouldn't be able to concentrate on her work. Several men, both brokers and clients, were angry and they acted. Inviting her to lunch, they gave her an envelope. It contained three things—two thousand dollars in cash, a round trip air ticket from Los Angeles to San Francisco and a list of appointments they had set up for job interviews in the Bay Area...as a stock broker! She went and was hired as the first woman broker on the West Coast for E.F. Hutton. Two years later, she was treated just like her fellow male brokers. She's still the proud owner of a gold belt buckle she received from the company for making over one hundred thousand dollars—just like the men got.

1978...*Robin Schumacher was a female accountant working in a small firm that her father once owned. "I worked my way up to senior accountant before hitting a brick wall. The men I worked with viewed me as weak, unable to make decisions, incompetent and something of a braggart. One fellow even asked me, 'Why aren't you home making babies like the rest of the women in this country? We men need these jobs.'"*

1981...Marilou soon started to wonder why some women had been able to become successful in careers that were originally channeled for males, such as airline pilots and dentists. During this period, she spent two years interviewing and photographing women who had chosen to become successful in jobs that did not involve nursing, teaching or hairdressing.

1981...Judith had started her own financial planning company four years previously. Business was good, revenues were growing and she was a respected member of her community. In the fall, she received a call from one of her bankers informing her of a "problem" and requesting her immediate presence the next morning at the bank. At the meeting, Judith learned that one of her partners, a woman, had raided a loan that Judith had personally guaranteed. Over $400,000 was missing—embezzled. The bank wanted its money. So did Judith. She never recovered any of the money from her former partner and friend. Over a period of time, she paid the bank back. In seeking the assistance of the local district attorney, she was brushed off and told that he didn't have time to enter into *women problems.*

That year changed Judith's life. The embezzlement sent her back to school, where she earned her doctorate in business administration by the end of the decade. Her dissertation focused on women's workplace relationships and sabotage within the workplace.

1983...*Good news! Women, trying to prove themselves, made significant headway in almost every occupation imaginable. Carol Spencer was a female pilot for a small shuttle company. It was difficult for her in the beginning...* "*Most of the men I worked with had serious problems relating to me. I don't think they could ever get used to a woman doing the kind of work that was traditionally reserved for men. Even the passengers looked frightened when they'd climb aboard. One woman turned to my supervisor and said, 'My God, is that really a woman up there in the cockpit? I'd rather wait for the next flight if you don't mind.' I eventually ended up getting the worst schedules and the worst routes.*"

1986...Marilou's husband's career necessitated a move from the East Coast to California in 1986. She secured a California teaching position and noted that many of the school administrators on the West Coast were women. This was totally unlike New York State. She asked the school principal, a woman, "How does this work? How do you get to be a principal? In New York all of the school principals are men."

The principal laughed and suggested that it would take a lot of hard work to obtain a position beyond the classroom. She also cautioned that the journey would not be without incident. "California is at the forefront for women in this country. However, just because you think you have the credentials to be a school administrator does not mean that *they* will bring you aboard. If you want to be a school administrator in this state, you'll have to take over a school that no one wants, or no one, even a man, can handle." Sobering words.

1986...Judith made a decision that she wanted to plunge full time into professional speaking and writing. Working on her dissertation as well as three separate and unrelated books on the topics of divorce, grieving and women and sabotage, she sold her company. Coming from a field where she earned fees and commissions, she never considered that there would be any gender disparity in the amount she would make. The wake-up call came when she quickly learned that male speakers made at least twice what women did. She also discovered that publishers were more likely to pay bigger advances to male business writers than they did to female writers. There were very few full-time women speakers and there were very few women business authors.

1988...Better news! Women were beginning to be a hot commodity in the world of business and administration. Stiff global competition changed the rules of business and how things were to be done. There was a new emphasis on teamwork, collaboration and consensus building. There were a great many jobs to be had and women were in high demand. Patricia Eldridge was hired as a financial consultant for a prestigious firm in Los Angeles: "I loved my job, even though I was making less than my male counterparts. I knew sooner or later the guys at the top would recognize my contributions. I believed that my exceptional job skills would eventually level the playing field, so to speak...It never happened. When a larger firm bought out our company, I saw the writing on the wall. I was one of the first people asked to leave."

1990...Marilou vowed to be different. Enrolling in the school of administration at California State University at Long Beach, she made a pact with herself: as a school administrator, she would not accept a position or school that no man would take. She completed the degree in two years and was promoted to the position of assistant principal of a middle school. One year later, a position was offered at one of the most renowned schools in California and she accepted. At that time, only 18 percent of all secondary school administrators were women. Marilou was on her way!

1990...Judith had finished her doctorate, had garnered global coverage for her seminal book, *Woman to Woman: From Sabotage to Support.* Every medium from *The Wall Street Journal, People* and the *National Enquirer* to CNN, *Oprah, Donahue* and *Geraldo* covered the book and she signed to be a national spokesperson for a Fortune 100 company. The *Chicago Tribune* selected *Woman to Woman* as the business book of the year. Judith was on her way (again)!

1993...Barbara Jensen was a highly qualified assistant director of a large computer manufacturing company. She was good at making important decisions for her company and her supervisors continued to write glowing reports about her success and performance at work. She could not, however, land a top seat in the corporation. One day she overheard two of her male colleagues talking in the copy room. "Barbara will never get that promotion over Bill. She just doesn't have what it takes to lead, she's not firm enough and she's does-n't have any guts... When people around here think of Barbara, they think of her in terms of the company 'mom' but not as someone who can make the tough decisions."

1994...As a school administrator, Marilou received several awards for her school including the California Distinguished School and National Blue Ribbon of Excellence. She was selected as a Johns Hopkins' Administrator of the Year. What accomplishments, she thought!! Commuting over two hours each day, she applied for a lateral move as a principal to several schools near her home. With her hard won credentials and awards, she theorized that any job she wanted would be hers. Was she wrong! In three different situations, an inexperienced young man was selected over her. What was the problem? She wasn't unqualified, unprofessional or socially inept. Indeed, as a highly qualified professional woman with *outstanding* credentials, she *should* have received at least one of those positions. Marilou began to wonder...*what's wrong with this picture?*

1994...Judith continued to write and speak. She and her work had been featured on over 500 radio and television programs. After completing a multi-year contract with another Fortune 100 company (that had recently merged with another giant), she submitted her final invoice...and was stiffed! Over $40,000 was owed. At the same time, she learned that there were men spokespersons that had been paid everything they billed. She contacted the president of the company after she had gotten encouragement from others who had been on the original team—he would do the right thing. Others told her that the company had gotten more publicity and coverage from her work than they ever expected, the president had loved her work. Within days, she was contacted and threatened by the company's PR firm. If she didn't withdraw her demand for payment, submit a formal apology, she would never work for a major company again. Judith began to wonder...*what's wrong with this picture?*

1995...*Susan McDonald was up for a promotion at work. She was the top candidate for the assistant controller position in a large manufacturing corporation. One of the men on the interview team leaked to Susan's coworkers that* *she had come across in the interview as a real braggart. He confessed: "Susan was definitely the best person for the job, but we perceived her recounting of her accomplishments as just plain bragging and it totally unnerved most of the men on the screening committee."*

1997... One evening while having dinner with a friend, Marilou complained about losing out on three positions to men with lesser experience or credentials. Her friend, a successful African-American male executive, tried to share some perspective. He argued that maybe her reason for not being selected had to do with a type of *dissonance.* "*Dissonance,*" she queried, "whatever is that?"

He began to explain that whenever he goes into a grocery store to shop, he encounters a recurrent problem. As he walks down an aisle with his shopping cart, he notices that often a white female will look over at him out of the corner of her eye. She looks at him...then glances back at her purse in the shopping cart. She immediately pulls her purse closer to herself, continuing to do so as she passes by his cart. "This is racial dissonance," her friend said. "The white woman does not realize that she has been socialized to think that I (the black man) may steal her purse. If you questioned her about it, she would deny that she had ever done anything to protect her purse from me. Her behavior and feelings are *subconscious.* She really does not know on the surface what made her clutch her purse as I passed by her grocery cart."

He suggested that men exhibit the same type of *dissonance* toward women. Men and women have different characteristics, behaviors and social expectations. And even though the gender dissonance may be in the man's subconscious, he reacts to it.

These new ideas served as a springboard for Marilou's research on women's issues and personal power issues.

1998... The headlines about Monica Lewinsky and Linda Tripp were everywhere. Sabotage, betrayal and conflicts were hot topics once again. Judith had a telephone conversation with the publisher of *Woman to Woman* and the idea of creating a new study that looked at current workplace behaviors of women was birthed, resulting in *Woman to Woman 2000.* Was Linda Tripp's covert taping of Monica Lewinsky an isolated incident, or were women actively betraying and setting other women up? It was time to re-address the issue of women re-address the issue of women undermining, sabotaging and bullying other women, which her previous studies had revealed were women's preference to avoid conflict, and to probe the issue of toxic mentors and create an effective roadmap to confront and communicate more effectively.

From her previous work, Judith knew that women exhibit *conscious* and *subconscious dissonance* toward other women. Women routinely say that they are totally supportive of other women, yet in many cases, their actions speak louder than their words. What an inspiration— Linda Tripp became Judith's example of the Saboteur of the Decade (beating out Tonya Harding)! Judith thought she had another major behavior discovery.

Where Now?
Where does the timeline take us next? Neither of us has a crystal ball. We both have years of experience that tells us nothing is resolved instantly. In evolutions and revolutions that involve behavior traits, it can take time—sometimes decades—to bring up the awareness levels so that effective change can be implemented. Once that awareness level is reached, women can begin to modify those behaviors that are causing them problems in achieving the success—and power—to which they are entitled. We like to call this "outsmarting" the SeXX Factor. Throughout this book, you will find triggers, pointers and examples from real experiences that we have lived through or discovered in our research and which will tremendously shortcut your learning curve.

Consider this book your primer and read on.

My God…is that really a woman in the cockpit?

– Airline passenger

Look over there—a female soccer coach! What were they thinking?

– Father of a team member

2

Prejudices:
Everyone Has Them!

Quickly—when you hear the word prejudice, what do you think? If you are like most people, it's just one thing—race...Black vs. White (or Hispanic, Asian, Arabic, etc.). And you are wrong...limited in your scope. Prejudice comes in all shapes and sizes and transcends multiple areas—think age, think sexism, think discrimination, think religion, think looks, think children, think marriage, think (<u>fill in the blank</u>).

Prejudice is woven throughout society—no place is excluded. During the first President Bush's Administration, former Senator John Tower was nominated for Secretary of Defense. Washington was abuzz about his alleged womanizing and drinking. Tower was invited to be on *This Week with David Brinkley*. Brinkley was away and veteran journalist Sam Donaldson stepped in as host. He said, "Well, Senator, it's not just alcohol, you know, there have been charges of womanizing." Tower responded, "I'm a single man; I do date women," and then added, "What's your definition of womanizing, Sam?"

Cokie Roberts was sitting there with a quasi-amused expression on her face listening to the exchange. Donaldson turned to her and said, "Cokie, do you have a definition of the term?" Her response was, "Well, I think most women know it when they see it, Senator."

And so it goes with prejudice...most women know it when they see it. When individuals harbor prejudices that are out of sync with reality, whether those prejudices come out in the workplace, in the academic world, in family life, they distort relationships or perceptions and can be detrimental to women. Many of the reactions and dissonance that men generate toward women can be the result of prejudices—pre-conceived and learned.

The Prejudice Factor:
An attitude that is preconceived and usually based on either a personal experience or the opinions passed on from others. Prejudices are rarely favorable or positive and can be directed toward an individual's or group's race, gender, culture, lifestyle or religion. Prejudice is directly linked to the SeXX Factor as the underlying cause of gender dissonance.

Key "isms" that women have had to deal with include racism, sexism, ageism and "good looksism." All are factors within the SeXX Factor. They are all bad news, but two of them, sexism and good looksism are a deadly duo. According to Cherokee Principle Chief Wilma Mankiller, sexism is very old. Before she was elected the first deputy chief of the Oklahoma tribe, she endured vicious opposition and distrust for eleven years. Mankiller says,

> *Sexism is not a Native American concept. When the Europeans arrived in America, Cherokee women living in the Southeast were consulted on major issues, attended councils and had an equal vote. The tribe's creator was called the Mother-Of-All-Nations and men and women lived in harmony.*
>
> *With the arrival of the Europeans—pilgrims—Indian women began marrying white settlers. Where they had been participants in councils in the past, their new spouses expected them to be quiet. The tribes creation story was altered and acculturation assigned women to secondary roles.*

The Workplace's Dirty Little Secret

"Good looksism" is blatant. Just ask former CBS morning personality, Kathleen Sullivan. In 1994, she resurfaced as spokesperson for Weight Watchers prior to its current spokesperson, Sarah Ferguson. Before her re-emergence, Sullivan had been unceremoniously dumped by CBS because of three well-publicized factors: she'd gained weight, she'd gotten a divorce and, horror of horrors, she'd let her hair go gray.

Her new position got the media's attention. All of a sudden, she was in *People* magazine, wanted by the talk shows and people returned her calls. An interview on Tom Snyder's CNBC show revealed that her exile had been very painful and that she was making money by teaching at golf clinics for women. Watching her interact with Snyder and take calls from listeners, you would be deeply impressed with her intelligence, her wit and her spontaneity and wonder why any television network would want to let this talent go.

Prejudice based on a person's looks is the workplace's dirty little secret. Unfortunately, women across the country experience this as a fact of life. It is quite common for employers to keep a negative stereotype or opinion about race and gender to themselves. When stereotypes about looks surface, they seem to be more acceptable than other stereotypes. Discrimination against overweight women is the most rampant form of this.

Esther Rothblum, Ph.D. is a professor at the University of Vermont and researches attitudes about obese people. One of her studies found that 60 percent of obese women and 30 percent of moderately overweight women reported that they had not been hired or not been promoted because of their weight. One woman in her study reported that she had gained ninety pounds after she had been put on steroids for a hand injury. When she appeared for interviews, she was rejected. The comments were, "She wasn't right for the position," or "The position has already been filled."

Hypocrisy Is Alive and Too Well
Women's weight matters more than men's. Most employment experts say that overweight men are more likely to be hired than overweight women. Terri Smith-Croxton is president of J. D. and Associates, an executive search firm in Arlington, Texas. She reported that she had sent a female candidate, who was well-groomed but overweight, for a position. They didn't hire her because her weight was a problem. Smith-Croxton says that they then asked to set up an interview with a male candidate whose resume had been sent. When she told them he was heavier than the female candidate they had just seen, their response was, "That's okay, as long as he's neat."

Unfortunately, many employers view an overweight man as someone who doesn't feel his looks are important or as being without vanity, but when it comes to women, they assume an overweight woman is lazy and has little or no self-control. In the eighties, Judith lived in the Bay Area of Northern California. One of the most visible corporate women during that time was Debi Coleman, then vice president at Apple Computer and the mastermind behind the restructuring of the manufacturing plant that enabled the Macintosh line to get on track. Coleman was a big player in the success of Apple's major product.

One of the Bay area's papers, the *San Jose Mercury News,* ran an extensive profile on her. Yes, there was mention of her work at Apple and her contribution to the overall success and the bottom line financial picture. But, the thrust of the article was more on Coleman's battle of the bulge. Several pictures accompanied the multi-page article, including one of her peering into an open refrigerator.

Women in the community were furious. The article did not focus on Coleman's accomplishments and her genius, but rather on her looks. Many of them cancelled their subscriptions. Would a successful man be profiled this way? Never!

In 1993, the Harvard School of Public Health surveyed over ten thousand young adults over a seventeen-year period and found overweight women pay a price for their poundage. The report, published in the *New England Journal of Medicine* in 1993, says obese women were 10 percent more likely to have incomes below the poverty level.

No matter how well they did in intelligence tests, fat women earned $6,710 less a year than other women with the same credentials and job skills. And women who are overweight are vulnerable to being fired, even though the Americans with Disabilities Act covers obesity. In Rhode Island, a federal discrimination suit was upheld in 1993, allowing a 320 pound woman to get her job back.

Overweight people aren't the only victims of this "good looksism" nonsense. Employers also see women with gray hair and assume she is not modern, up-to-date on current trends or able to use a computer. The opposite can also hold true. You may be young or look young and find yourself rejected for a position you are well qualified for. A study has shown that tall men have employment preference over short men.

Innuendos Out of Place
When Judith joined E.F. Hutton in the early seventies as the sole woman stockbroker in the Palo Alto, California, office, she didn't have

one client. Within two years, she was one of the top brokers nationally, earning her a private office.

At that time, she recalled her manager saying he wouldn't hire any other women to be brokers, because he "knew" how women were with other women. He ate his words a year later, when another woman came on board. Judith also distinctly remembers comments about the way she would build her client base from other brokers—all men. It was routine to hear innuendoes like, "Well, I'm sure she'll be successful in getting and building clients—we all 'know' how she will do it."

Judith admits to being quite naive back in those days. The only way she knew how to do "it" was to work hard, long hours, prospect, and, hopefully, make recommendations that were successful for the clients who, in turn, would increase their business and refer other clients to her. She thought that was how the game was played.

The innuendos that were made flew over her head at the time. If she had known back then what she knows today, the sexist comments from coworkers and managers would have been countered. And, she would have understood the SeXX Factor was at work here. She was working longer hours than the men did and they resented her for doing it and bypassing them in personal production.

Nancy, a successful agent working in insurance, also had a similar experience. The second year that she was in the business, she made the Million-Dollar Round Table. The percentage of women who make it is very low in comparison to the men. She told us:

> When I went to my first meeting, I was shocked to see all the male faces. Of approximately four thousand attending, an estimated two hundred were women. As I walked down the hall, I would be congratulated, but with a surprised look—as if, 'How could she possibly achieve this?' For the men, it was just assumed that they would achieve the Round Table. Prizes included navy blue sports coats and company insignia rings, and the activities were all jock related.

Sometimes the dissonance that is displayed when women enter areas that have previously been dominated by men is expressed in the form of exclusion—prizes are not attractive to women and outside events and activities at gatherings are typically for the men. Judith remembers a time when she won a prize at E.F. Hutton—the classic navy blue coat with special brass buttons. Her manager realized that it wasn't appropriate so he told her to pick out another jacket she would like. She did and gave him the bill for five hundred dollars!

Everyone Has Prejudices

Many believe we live in a color-blind, gender-blind society. Nonsense. To have that belief puts one in la-la land; it's just plain ignorance. Everyone is not on an equal footing. Someday, we will routinely judge people solely on the basis of their characters and the quality of the individual, but it hasn't happened yet.

Any time we allow ourselves to be pulled into stereotyping a culture, race or gender, it becomes easy to regress to overt prejudice. Think about it. It is not difficult to place cultures, races and religions into a common stereotype. Just as is the SeXX Factor, prejudice is usually learned and frequently subconscious.

So What if Men Are Uncomfortable with Women's Behavior?

Not so what—we should care because men's discomfort with certain female behaviors has a direct impact on the status of women—it doesn't matter if it's in the workplace, at home or in a social environment. Granted, women have made strides in the workplace, but statistics indicate that it will likely take us another one hundred years to achieve equal parity with men in corporate and professional arenas.

Currently, here's where we stand in the workplace:

- Women hold only 8 percent of the top CEO positions in the U.S.
- Women earn more than 50 percent of all bachelors and masters degrees, and 33 percent of the master degrees are in business administration.
- Fewer than 10 percent of the top officers in the nation's 500 largest companies are women.
- Today, women comprise less that 20 percent of the nation's architects, 10 percent of clergy and engineers, 3 percent of technicians and 5 percent of senior management (those of the title of vice-president and above). Women comprise 83 percent of librarians, 86 percent of elementary school teachers, 88 percent of speech therapists, 94 percent of registered nurses and 99 percent of kindergarten teachers, preschool teachers, dental hygienists and secretaries.

Most women feel that the advancement of women in the workplace in senior management is just too slow. Because of the small percentage of women at the top in the corporate workplace, women have created their own game plans—they've left traditional workplaces. Consider this:

- In 2002, there were an estimated 6.2 million privately-held, women-owned firms, employing 9.2 million people and generating in excess of $1.2 trillion in sales.
- Women-owned firms are not just in service industries. They are expanding into construction, manufacturing and transportation.
- The workforce of women-owned firms shows more gender equity. Overall, they employ a balanced workforce (52 percent women, 48 percent men), while men business owners employ 38 percent women and 62 percent men.

The statistics related reflect the enormous monetary value of women-owned businesses. The workplace in the form of Corporate America has had a steady flow of incredible talent exiting its doors. It can't afford to lose more women.

The $1,000,000 Question:
Should Women Change Their Behavior?
Your new awareness of the SeXX Factor is not all about changing behavior; rather it's about controlling and monitoring the amount of gender dissonance created in the workplace for your *own* sake. It's about changing your attitude, and in some cases, your behavior as well.

Outsmarting The SeXX Factor
Qualified men have always had access to power. Women can now increase their likelihood of attaining power and position. Women already at the top know that men in power continually do what it takes to keep their position. They are in control, they are determined, they've got all the right moves and they recognize what's required to capture and keep the power.

Successful women already at the top have understood this same principle, they just didn't have a label for it, a terminology. These women have become aware of the SeXX Factor and are mindful of its effect and impact on men. They know that if they confuse, frustrate or annoy those who have power over them, they in turn will lose out on chances to gain power. Their awareness of gender dissonance has enabled these powerful women to even the playing field to achieve the success they deserve.

I find women's fascination with jewelry completely unfathomable. Ditto with shoes. And blabbing for hours about someone's new hair do. What a waste of time. Oh, and another thing—when a woman and a man have a little problem or altercation, instead of going to the man later to deal with the problem, the woman usually goes to all available women in the vicinity to get a group effort going against the guy. My reaction to that is "Get some intestinal fortitude and say what you have to say to the person directly!"

– George, District Manager,
husband and father

3

The Gender Dissonance Factor:
Men, Women and the
Eternal Battle of the Sexes

Dissonance, conflict and disharmony go hand-in-hand. Most people think of conflict as being openly visible. Yet, too often, it's not—conflict and disharmony are more likely to be felt, as something "in the air," before either can out-rightly be pointed at.

Does *gender dissonance* really have an effect on women who want to interact successfully with men in personal encounters and in business? Why is it that women could break through identified barriers to advance to mid-level positions, but cannot reach the top posts in business, management, politics or education? Could this dissonance be holding women back from reaching private goals or getting hired at any level within an organization? What about community activities and association projects—are there invisible barriers and roadblocks that haven't been identified as such?

The Gender Dissonance Factor
The subconscious discomfort, uneasiness or anger that men may feel when they work or interact with women.

Let's look at the differences between men and women. When men and women interact and their perceptions support one another, they are in a consonant relationship. But if men and women sense each other differently due to differences in roles, their interchange will be fraught with friction. Since, in this book, we are looking at men's perception of women and how this affects us, we will focus on this. Due to men's problematic perceptions like gender styles (she acts too masculine), communication styles (she brags too much) or cultural expectations (she wants privileges at work for being a working mother), conflicts of interest can arise. These conflicts can result in situations of tension between men and women.

Dissonance...Men in power positions were surveyed regarding this tension or *dissonance*. Results from these conversations generated by hundreds of men were telling. Do you recognize any of the behaviors and actions they cite?

> *For ages "strong men" have used a stoic expression to convey power. But it doesn't usually work for women. A woman's ability to mirror and convey approachability and empathy can be a valuable edge in business. Don't act like a man when you are not a man.*

> *I felt **angry** when my fellow committee member, a woman, made me look bad in public.*

> *Perhaps I'm old fashioned, but I really hate to see women asserting themselves by being vulgar, attempting toughness.*

> *I became **frustrated** when a woman member talked on and on in a PTA meeting.*

> *Getting too serious too quickly during meetings annoys me. Some women think they have to be so "manly" and down to business that they miss the point that we are still just people trying to get a job done. Some intelligent sense of humor would help both genders, frankly.*

> *Too many times, women only want the condensed version, then they give a premature opinion before hearing all the facts even on a complex issue. "Not sure I understand, but here's what I think..."*

> *When a woman uses sexual stuff to relate to me personally at work...I've got to admit...that's confusing information to deal with.*

> *Using flirtation as a tool to get what women want really pushes my buttons. This sometimes is only obvious to the observer(s). The*

male heads of organizations either choose not to see it, or like it any-
way, because guys are too often insecure in their own skin.

I was really mad when she got the job I thought I was going to get.

I can't stand inattentive drivers. Although both men and women
do this, I seem to notice it more with women. I always lament getting
stuck behind the "purse digger at the stop light." For some reason these
women believe that a stop light is a signal to start digging in their
purses. All too often they're still digging when the light turns green...

A coworker did something at work that made me look exception-
ally bad in front of my boss. Okay, I'll admit she's good at what she
does, but her actions just weren't fair.

Marilou wondered if there were gender differences between men
and women that caused males to experience *dissonance* that, in turn, led
to the SeXX Factor. It led her to her original theory, and she began her
research. We broadened this research into private and professional
spheres in which women and men were interviewed. It suggested that
women needed to become more aware of what causes men to experience this feeling, this dissonance. Why? Because all agreed: These
behaviors are keeping women from successful interactions with men.

The SeXX Factor *subconsciously* causes discomfort for many men.
They would like the feeling to stop, but they don't know what's causing
it. They do know, however, that these feelings are generated from the
presence of women. The SeXX Factor should be considered one of the
most pervasive obstacles women presently face when seeking advancement in their careers and successful interchanges in their family and private domains.

Are the Dissonance Factor and SeXX Factor New?
Over forty years ago, Betty Friedan published *The Feminine Mystique.* It was
the first book to reveal that there were barriers or obstacles preventing
women's access to power. The Women's Movement marks its birth with
her controversial book that changed the lives of both working-for-pay
and working-for-no-pay women. Using Friedan's book as a springboard,
many women were able to jump hurdles and barriers that previously prevented them from reaching success. Included were issues that involved
lack of confidence, lack of money or lack of aspiration:

Issue	Cause
I can't get (or do) the job	Low confidence
My husband won't let me	Unwilling to challenge role or authority
No one likes me	Paranoia and low self-esteem
I can't...I have to fix dinner	Home and family responsibilities
I can't afford to take classes or get my degree	Lack of money

Since Friedan's groundbreaking book, thousands of books have been written to further clarify the roadblocks to equality for women. Some of the new problems are:

Issue	Cause
My children's coaches won't take my suggestions	Gender dissonance
I can't relocate	Lack of mobility
The job is too dangerous	Sex-role stereotyping
The director, manager or VP is a woman, but doesn't know I'm alive	Lack of mentors
I never see women managers in my department or unit	Lack of role models
There are no women in upper management; thus I can't make it to the top	Glass ceiling
I can't raise my voice or yell	Sex-role stereotyping
There aren't any good schools	Lack of opportunity locally
I have to dress (look) better than the men do	Discrimination ("looksism")
I'm not a jock, I don't golf	Limited access to networking

As the causes of inequality have revealed themselves over the years, women continue to struggle for clear passages to power and successful interactions with men. There always seems to be obstacles. Women and men work and play with different sets of rules—some written, but many unwritten.

Women Have Made Gains, But...

Women *are* making tremendous progress toward getting top power career positions. Look at all the women senators—filling more than 10 percent of the Senate in 2002. Check out Olympia Snowe, Elizabeth Dole, Dianne Feinstein or Hillary Rodham Clinton, Sandra Day O'Connor and Christine Todd Whitman...senators, Supreme Court Justice and a governor turned EPA Administrator.

In the national election of 2000, either of the major parties could have positioned a female vice president candidate on the slate—Dianne Feinstein on the Democratic side and Christine Todd Whitman on the Republican side were the most visible and logical choices. Both highly qualified, yet both passed over as a choice by both women and men who were in power positions to make "it" happen. Prior to his death in 1998, former Senator Barry Goldwater expressed that there were many women qualified to be President—and once one gets on an elected ticket, there's nothing to hold her back!

The good news is that women have overcome internal and external barriers and are making choices to finally get to the top. The bad news, or rather the shocking truth, is women in government and in business *are still not* gaining access to top power positions. Why? Because men control who gets to the top, and it's most likely to be someone just like them.

When Judith was researching and writing *Woman to Woman*, she met one of the divisional IBM presidents on a plane trip from New York to San Francisco. He expressed interest in her work on the Sabotage Factors when she revealed that she was working on her doctorate. She thought it would be a great opportunity to get his input and, with his permission, interviewed him.

She asked him what he thought about today's working woman (the year was 1986). He said that "she" was terrific—bright, articulate, hard working, a real asset to the IBM team. Judith then asked him how many positions would be considered "senior management" in his division. His response, "How do you define senior management?"

Judith already knew the final response (zero), but continued anyway.

"To me, senior management would be anyone who reports directly to you and/or has a direct responsibility for a P&L. How many positions do you have that would fill that definition?"

"Ten," was his response.

"Tell me—how many women are in the ten?"

"None."

She continued, "When do you think women will attain senior management status within IBM?"

"At least five years from now," was his response.

Judith then took the drink napkin and drew a pyramid. She told him that in positioning him at the tip of the pyramid as the president, the immediate section below—senior managers—were all men. Below them, she drew two more layers with the third being a mix of middle managers and the bottom various support staff. Pointing out the differences, she said, "You have just told me, a stranger, that you have ten senior positions, all filled by men, and that women will not be in any one of them for at least five years."

"Here's what is happening," the man explained. "The men know that they don't have to compete with any of the women, at least for five years. The women, though, on a long shot are going to attempt a breakthrough of some sort before your projected timeframe—five years can be a long time when one is ambitious. But, they have an added challenge. Not only do they have to compete with the men, they have to compete with each other; they know damn well that only one of them is going to get the nod. The result is that women will most likely end up undermining other women to get to bat first." A dissonance within the workplace.

He was right, it was five years later that IBM propelled a woman into senior management.

The Glass Ceiling—Yesterday and Today

The *glass ceiling* metaphor continues to explain the scarcity of women in upper management positions. First introduced in 1987 with Ann Morrison's book, *Breaking the Glass Ceiling*, women finally had a term to describe the transparent barrier that prevented them from rising to certain levels in corporate America. Today, the *glass ceiling* is used to describe internal types of barriers (*I could never pass the law exam*) and external types of barriers (*I've got four kids and a husband*). The *glass ceiling*, placed there by men, needed to be crashed through if women were ever going to get to the top. Its introduction to the workplace vocabulary in 1987 answered some questions and gave a name to what many women experienced.

...and the Muddy Bottom

In Judith's study that looked at five thousand women in the general workplace, she learned that the great majority of women (89 percent) didn't strive to be in top management. Their workplace issues focused on pay inequities (which the glass ceiling issue also addresses), communicating more effectively, being in balance, not undermining themselves nor being undermined and sabotaged by others and, most importantly, prejudice with an emphasis on sexism and looksism (see chapter 5). Let's face it, a man can be ugly, he can be overweight, his clothing and appearance can be out of whack and few will fault him. If a woman has a run in her stockings, her makeup is misapplied (or non-existent, for that matter), her clothes are a little too tight, or she appears frumpy, she'll get dinged from all sides.

In many arenas, women still get stuck at lower level jobs. Power is a player at the top—men usually are in the final decision-making positions and if there is something that bugs them about a woman's behavior or mannerisms, it becomes a factor in present and future decision making. Nevertheless, women have power, plenty of it. And, it sometimes holds them back.

Using Your Awareness of the Dissonance Factor
If women act a certain way, such as using profanity or gossiping, this could trigger men's feelings of discomfort, frustration and annoyance.

This is the enemy within, so to speak—I can be my own worst enemy. Most likely, women believe that hard work and perseverance will eventually get them to the top power positions. Yet they've been unaware that certain behaviors and habits, many of which are linked to traditional female upbringing and traits, can cause men to experience the SeXX Factor. A new awareness of this will be an essential ingredient to gain power at work and successfully interact with men in everyday life.

Outsmarting The SeXX Factor
Becoming aware of the SeXX Factor and managing its effect on men is not about trying to make men feel better. It's about acting the same way that men have done for years—doing whatever it takes to be successful and get to the top. Once you gain access to power positions, you can begin to change the culture that exists at the top for all women. The basic principles to gain access to power are simple—here's how:
- Develop awareness of those behaviors, actions, situations or events that prompt men to experience the SeXX Factor.
- Use your new awareness to manage the effects of the SeXX Factor that could ultimately limit your access to power.

In Judith's IBM example, it was clear the company knows what it needs. It needs everything that men, in particular, are doing and have been doing for the past two hundred years. Men have learned how to gain access and manage power. Women can now become aware of and focus on one last obstacle, that of the SeXX Factor and how it may impact their access to power and successful interaction with men. Then, the sky really does become the limit.

When women become mindful of the factors that prompt those at the top (men) to feel uneasy or unsettled when they interact with female power figures, they can channel or mitigate these obstacles. For example, men become confused when they try to equate things that women do. Gossiping...*lack of trust*...Crying...*pleading*. These types of behaviors, associated with female traits, cause men to feel uneasy, angry, unsettled or frustrated. As a result, men at the top have *subconsciously* denied women access to power.

Throughout the following chapters you will learn that actions such as miscommunicating, overtly bragging, flaunting too much confidence and excluding men from discussions can limit your own chances for success. Descriptive and expressive interviews with high-ranking men and women from such organizations as Mattel, Mobile Oil and Epson America as well as men and women in pivotal positions affecting one's children and home life reveal that it is often seemingly inconsequential conduct that results in stagnation, that prevents women from attaining the success we deserve.

This book shatters currently conceived notions about why we fail to interact successfully and accomplish our goals. It offers women practical strategies enabling them to rise above gender politics and move forward on the path to success.

If you haven't taken the SeXX Factor short quiz on page 6, do it now. It will help you identify some of the behaviors that drive men crazy and create gender dissonance. Whether it's pleading, gossiping too much, talking without thinking or overly apologizing, the result may be your male boss's or colleague's frustration and anger. Whatever the arena, gender dissonance creates problems and impedes progress and the accomplishment of one's goals, whether they are to aid a child in prospering in school, to gain benefits for a worthy cause or to climb to the top at work.

Power comes in many forms. Women must learn to use it properly.

– Dana, Criminal Law Attorney

4

The Power Factor:
Don't Overuse It

The SeXX Factor is about us as women and how we affect men who hold some form of power over us in our personal lives and in the workplace. Men's and women's differences in roles (she's too timid to manage others), differences in communication styles (she talks too much) or differences in cultural expectations (she likes to decorate her office) often cause tension or dissonance on the part of men.

Men in positions of power often feel uncomfortable when they interact with women who behave in ways that are not associated with power. We have called this "power static," because the messages that are passed between such men and women are garbled and unclear. Men are usually very *unaware* of what causes the SeXX Factor. They *are* aware, however, that they don't like what they feel—*the dissonance*—and thus avoid feeling this way at all costs. In such situations, what is the impact for and on women? In order to avoid the discomfort, men in power will prevent women from getting ahead, from breaking into their world, so to speak. This becomes a very costly occurrence for women.

The Power Factor:
Actions taken by someone in a position of power and directed at another who is perceived to have less influence and authority.

In the mid-eighties, Janet Hagberg's book *Real Power* was published. It identified six stages of power—from Total Powerlessness to Power by Gestalt. These stages fit into where many women are today and include:

Stage One—Powerless. You feel trapped. All power is outside of you and the only power that you might have is via manipulation. This is expressed in forms of whining, threatening, withholding favors, passive-aggressive behaviors, sabotage and the like. Women in the muddy bottom are stuck here.

It's not uncommon to feel insecure, dependent, low on self-esteem, uninformed and helpless, but not hopeless. What moves you out of it is to develop and expand your self-esteem and your skills. The biggest thing that holds one back is fear. This is the time to reach out: forge networks, find allies, get support, expand your skills, appreciate yourself, confront your fears, take responsibility, talk with your boss, change jobs if you need to, get out of an abusive relationship if there is one, and, most of all, confront yourself. What enables movement to the next stage is confidence.

Stage Two—Power By Association. You've got enough skills to become a part of a group, whether it is medicine, sales, clerical, sports—you've mastered it and fit into a culture and become a player—you're one of the gang. When in this stage, you don't like to see people break out. If you see someone raising her head and becoming a leader, you or the group becomes tough on her. You pull her down because it would be a threat to the group if she left—the crab in the basket scenario. It's the muddy bottom again.

The power game that gets played is, "Let's make a deal. You do this for me, I'll do that for you." This should be better known as a win-lose negotiation, not win-win, unless it's a win-win in the sense that we all hang in together and no one moves on and up or out. A vision for long-term growth is blocked.

In corporate America, you are inclined to find *more women in Stage Two,* than men. Men move out of the second stage as fast as possible. The characteristics of this stage include learning the ropes and the culture, being dependent upon supervisors and leaders and, at the same time, creating a new self-awareness.

Overall, there is a stay-put attitude with a slight nudge of wanting to move on. The need for security and lack of confidence are the two primary ingredients that hold someone back. Ways to move on include finding a mentor; getting feedback; being competent at the skills you have; expanding your credentials or getting new credentials; becoming more involved; taking risks; expanding your network; taking care of yourself; doing something on your own, taking on the masculine model (this is temporary) if necessary and working out any negative or hold-back relationships.

Stage Three—Power by Symbols. Men usually get stuck in this stage. When women reach it, they try to pass through it very quickly. The third stage is what Hagberg calls the *dynamo stage* or *control stage.* The transition from this stage is done from what Judith calls the *cosmic goose*—a situation or event that has happened that, if you had your druthers, you would not want it to repeat. But, from it, growth occurs.

Power by symbols is perfect for Baby Boomers—they tend to measure their success/power by the number of items-toys-titles, etc. they have. It can mean, "I've got mine, I'm happy, but I want more." It is the accumulation of whatever counts in your particular group. It could be college degrees, credentials, even a certain type of car.

At some point, the question surfaces, "What is life about?" You end up redefining what power means to you and start thinking more long-term. No longer are you guided by a "What's in it for me?" and a "What will I lose?" attitude. Instead, you ask, "What can I give?"

Characteristics include egocentricity as well as being realistic and competitive. Individuals in the third stage are experts, ambitious and often charismatic. The area that is a hold-back is not knowing that you're stuck or there are greater things in a cosmic sense. The crisis that usually moves you forward is the cosmic goose.

Two movies stand out as examples of the cosmic goose. In *The Doctor,* starring William Hurt, Hurt is a fast-track whiz, an egocentric surgeon who develops cancer of the throat—the cosmic goose. After a series of traumatic events, he eventually recovers and turns around—for the better—in his personal life and teaching style within the hospital.

In *Regarding Henry,* Harrison Ford is a no-nonsense lawyer who is shot—the cosmic goose. Through his slow recovery, he comes to realize that some of the cases that he successfully argued and represented were unethical. He sets out to sort out the wrong he has done via his legal skills and, at the same time, as the good doctor did, gets his family and life back in balance.

Ways to move beyond this stage include learning to be alone, reflecting on yourself; trying new things that make you think; doing things differently; developing relationships and obtaining support from individuals in Stages Four, Five and Six; continuing to expand networks; concentrating on the present and being reflective.

The Fourth Stage—Power by Reflection. This can best be described as a sandwich stage and one of influence. This stage often drives men crazy because it is too passive—remember, they love the Power of Symbols Stage, Stage Three. Moving from there into reflection means quiet time.

This stage is tough. You finally stop and really ask questions and start looking for answers. Egos get in the way—some feel a loss of personal power and self. They may even regress to prior stages, until the cosmic goose hits.

Life experiences count—you are older, wiser and have some wisdom. The issue becomes, *How do you train yourself to be able to use power well and have the strength to hold onto it?*

Mentoring becomes a factor—not you reaching up to someone to mentor you; rather you reaching out to mentor another. You recognize that there are issues far bigger than just you. You get held back when you don't feel a real need for new life purposes. The way you move forward is to let go of your ego.

The Fifth Stage—Power by Purpose. This stage is supported by vision and passion. Common characteristics of this stage include calmness and humbleness; being a visionary; being self-accepting; feeling purposeful; being comfortable in allowing others to stretch and reach; making mistakes; being competent in life and expanding spirituality.

The only way you can lose this type of power is when you spend years at it and never feel you are making headway. Or, you are driven out of the community, such as being discredited in some way which would be very painful or hard on you. With your discreditation, your cause is discredited.

With highly publicized business scandals (Arthur Anderson, Enron, Qwest, Tyco, etc.), an example of a company which practices Stage Five is Ben and Jerry's Ice Cream. Ben and Jerry put limits on what they can earn in relation to their lowest paid employees. Companies are now scrambling to do "good deeds" for their communities and their employees...not just the executives.

What holds people back is their lack of faith and the feeling that they have too much to lose if they follow their passions and visions—even if they believe it to be their true sense of purpose.

The Sixth Stage—Power by Gestalt. This stage is like the wise old soul. Its characteristics include being unafraid of paradoxes, unafraid of death and practicing highly ethical behavior. You are beyond the need to exercise power—because of your very nature, you in effect, have power—and you are often quiet in your overall service. Mother Teresa was a classic example. It's a stage that few achieve.

Doing It Right

Power is part of everyday life. Getting anything done, whether at home or at work, involves some form of power. We've identified fifteen factors of power from others' experiences. Included are:

Recognition

By saying "thanks," the person you thank becomes a friend for life. Writing thank you notes and even taking detours to be able to thank and recognize others, lets people know that you care. It can never be overdone.

Showing Up

A five minute, face-to-face meeting can cinch a deal or smooth over a torrential fiasco. Sports agent and legend Mark McCormack states that it is frequently worth hopping on a plane and flying three thousand miles for a meeting that only lasts a few minutes.

Timely Calls

Don't let things fester. Most major problems today start from a small disturbance. Making and returning phone calls makes all the difference.

Minutiae

Get the facts, know the facts and understand the facts. If you don't, the little stuff can eliminate you from the running.

Rolodex-PDA

Author and CEO Harvey Mackay says that your sphere of influence is directly proportional to the thickness of your rolodex or PDA.

Work the phones, go to cocktail parties. Not only is it what you know, but who you know.

Homework
Knowledge is power. Find out the details of what makes customers, managers, co-workers, even opponents, click and tick.

Credibility
Be honest and have all your facts together. Get input from others, especially from those "in the know." Avoid "rumorisms"—those gems that are diluted as well as inflated traveling along the workplace grapevine.

Commitment
Almost anyone can sense your emotional—or lack of it—commitment. You don't have to be in the same room. It is the passion and tone you carry in your voice that does it. As one of our interviewees said, the last thing he wants to do is waste his time fighting a fanatic. That strong emotional commitment can help you to carry the day in ever present workplace "battles."

Time Management
Stay focused and prioritize. By the end of each day, you should have found a way to work on one or two of your key issues.

Just Say NO
Don't do well what you have no business doing and do well what you have business doing.

Minding Your Manners
Be beyond reproach on the "little stuff," such as getting to meetings early, being on time, dressing appropriately, understanding the nuances of cultural diversity, etc. Ask yourself, *"What would my mother say/think?"*

Decency
Never show others up, never make them look foolish and treat others with respect. Otherwise, you will find yourself the target of a "don't get mad, get even" approach. You lose big time.

Discipline

The nation's roadway system is frequented by "Yield Right Of Way" signs. That's not restricted—the same thing holds within and outside of the workplace. You, in fact, may be right on a priority or assertion, but there will be times when you need to hold back or even back off and be prepared to come forward another day to fight for your cause.

Street Smarts

Take the path of least resistance and devote time to building your networks and allies within your workplace as well as outside. "Street Smarts" also means "Maintain Visibility." Don't assume that others will know that your work is great and creative. Sometimes, you have to tell them.

Results

Identify one single project upon which you want to put your signature stamp. Focus. Be myopic. Chisel away at the nuts and bolts.

Common Sense

Some have it, too many don't. Do your best to acquire some.

One of the hit movies in the early 90s starred Kathy Bates, Jessica Tandy, Mary Stuart Masterson and Mary Louise-Parker. It was adapted from the Fanny Flag novel, *Fried Green Tomatoes at The Whistle Stop Cafe.* In one of the most memorable scenes, Evelyn, Kathy Bates' character, is outraged when two young beauties in a Volkswagen cut in front of her and steal the parking space she has been waiting for. "Face it, we're younger and faster," they blithely tell her when she complains.

A transformation comes over the meek, compliant Evelyn. She yells out, "Twanda!" Calling forth her version of a gutsy female warrior, she then backs up her car and rams it into the back of the now empty Volkswagen. Not once, but six times. When the two young women rush out to the scene of automotive mayhem, she says, "Face it, girls, I'm older and I've got more insurance."

Although you wouldn't approve of a person ramming someone else's car, the point Kathy Bates' character made is critical. She called up her power and she took it. But only after her sense of fairness had been taken advantage of. You needn't wait, but do your homework before you need to call Twanda.

Outsmarting the SeXX Factor

Power is always a factor. The key is not to abuse it—consciously or sub-consciously.

Anna has what it takes to get to the top. She's smart, attractive and nice to be around. She could have been the next vice president if it wasn't for her baby talk... Whenever she wants something from a man around here, she does this baby-speak type of thing... "Wud you pwease help me..."

– Richard, Account Executive

5

The Cleavage Factor:
Misinterpretations of Sexuality

The workplace isn't perfect. Uncertainty exists about how to handle issues of sexuality for men who have traditionally viewed women only as wives or girlfriends and continues to cause men stress and discomfort on the job. Their uneasiness and lack of knowledge about sexuality in the workplace is not surprising. As a culture, we are not altogether comfortable with sexuality of any kind.

Consider Henry, a vice president of a manufacturing company:

> *I confess, I still look and think about women in sexual terms. It's not that I want to have sex with them, but I like looking and thinking to myself*—she looks good. *I like the feeling, but it can be a real distraction if an attractive, powerful woman comes aboard...It's confusing stuff.*

It isn't that men don't enjoy working with women. When surveyed, more men than women said that they had no preference as to whether they had a male or female boss. In fact, in repeated studies, more women said that they did not want a woman boss. In addition, men often confess that they enjoy intellectual pursuits with female colleagues as they do not customarily experience this with their wives.

After talking with hundreds of men on this topic, we've identified seven types of sexual interactions between men and women that often trigger the SeXX Factor.

1. Fair Play—Men's Worst Fear

Today's man at work definitely worries about sexual harassment. The law-suits and settlements have cost individuals and businesses mega billions over the years. Men who used to touch the arms of female colleagues no longer feel free to express what, to the men, was once a gesture of friend-liness. Men feel uncomfortable, because in their view the rules about what constitutes sexual harassment in the workplace are ambiguous.

As one man remarked, *"I've got to watch everything I say. I don't want to end up as a headline in my local newspaper."*

Most men interviewed said they feel like they're *"walking on eggshells"* most of the time. Sam, a high level administrator, disclosed an incident that involved a young female colleague. He noticed that her zipper was open on her pants suit and that he could see her underwear in full view. He was so nervous about the situation that, at first, he looked away and didn't mention it to her....

> *I didn't want her to think that I was even looking at her zipper for fear she'd think something about it. I kept thinking about it and finally said to myself, This is stupid. I called her into my office and told her about her zipper being open. We both laughed about it and got on with our jobs.*

Ironically, laws designed to prevent sexual harassment at work have actually hindered women's advancement in the workplace. They can demean a woman's status as a worker by putting an undue emphasis on sexual relationships rather than work relationships. Like the proverbial elephant in the room, the subject is in the back of every worker's mind. Although women rarely file sexual harassment claims against men in the workplace, a handful of cases have received extensive media cover-age and have helped to dramatize the possibility for men.

Some men worry that a remark or gesture made in innocence could be misconstrued as something sexual. Others have reported that they are "scared to death" they may be accused of sexual harass-ment. They feel like the deer caught in the headlights—they are damned if they do, damned if they don't.

Outsmarting the SeXX Factor

Initiate discussions with men at work regarding where you stand on the issue of sexual harassment. Let them know up front that you won't be offended if they compliment your new outfit or suggest that you look "great" on a particular day. To show that you're not a threat, send subtle suggestions that you're on "their side." A sample conversation might go something like this:

> **You:** *Joe, did you hear about the woman who just filed a sexual harassment claim against her boss in the California division?*

> **Joe:** *Yes. What's going on? I know David and I think he's innocent. He's told me that he's been worried about Susan for a long time.*

> **You:** *Interesting. Sexual harassment laws were originally designed for women workers in factories. They are important. . . but I think it's important not to jump to conclusions. Too often, laws are manipulated and abused—we read about it everyday.*
> *Joe, one thing I want you to know, I don't know if the charges are valid or not, but I want you to be comfortable working with me. I'm complimented when you tell me I look good in a particular outfit. I'm a big girl and if I think someone is coming on too strong, I let him know. I think most women are that way. Please know that sexual harassment should not be an issue between you and me.*

> **Joe:** *Thanks.*

---

2. Too Close for Comfort—It's Enough to Drive Him Wild

One female executive, LuAnn, disclosed that she used to call on one of her male colleagues when she needed help with a particular problem at work. Since they both had busy schedules and did not work at the same location, they would meet at a small pizza place after work to have a drink and trade notes. LuAnn was soon being asked by several of her female colleagues what she liked about the man. One brave soul even asked her if she was having an affair!

"Good grief," she complained, "have a few drinks with a guy and the entire company has you in bed."

While LuAnn's male colleague enjoyed her company, he began to worry about their relationship. LuAnn believed that he probably had always related to women in sexual terms and that his new relationship with her began to cause him some degree of uncertainty. For example, he always thought he had to pay for their drinks and food as if they were on a date. He later confided to her that his immediate supervisor had tried to ascertain whether he had something "going on the side."

Professional relationships between men and women are relatively new. Men often experience confusion, fear and frustration when they are forced to respond to woman in any context other than sexual.

John, an executive in a company that employs five hundred people, commented about his apprehension of female relationships at work:

> *I'm called on the carpet all the time by male coworkers whenever I'm seen alone with one of our female executives, especially the good-looking ones. I tell them this is business, but I know they're still wondering...*

Most of the professional men interviewed reported that being close to a female colleague in public caused them to experience sexual tension. In addition, they responded that the mere physical proximity of their presence together in public made them feel uncomfortable for fear of what people might think about them. They are concerned that peers would view their relationships with women as unseemly, which could later injure their professional reputations.

Outsmarting the SeXX Factor

Be aware that most career men are on guard with new male-female work relationships. Go out in public with groups of coworkers, keep the conversation light and refer to your new relationships as pure collegiality.

---

3. Goldie Hawn Doesn't Work Here Anymore

Men have been dealing with the *I'm so cute* and *Don't you just love me* type of comments and behavior from women their entire lives. When they interact with women at work who exhibit these types of mannerisms, they become very confused. They do not associate women who respond to them in this manner with power. Richard, an account executive, spoke about his confusion as he related to one particular woman at work:

> *Anna has what it takes to get to the top. She's smart, attractive and nice to be around. She could have been the next vice president if it wasn't for her baby talk... Whenever she wants something from a man around here, she does this baby speak type of thing... "Wud you pwease help me..."*

It's not what you'd expect from someone wanting a shot at the top. Not only do I feel sorry for her, but it also makes me feel real uncomfortable and irritated watching this.

A woman's cute and helpless behavior at work drives men nuts! Men generate negative feelings when they are forced to respond to this type of sexuality in the workplace. One executive reported that when he observes women using a stereotypical "cutesy" or sexy type of behavior rather than her mind to make a point, he simply doesn't know how to respond. Richard continued,

When a woman behaves like this...I don't know how to deal with the situation other than to revert to a typical male/female relationship.

Ray is a health care administrator. A woman playing cute is also a trigger for him:

One mannerism that grates on me and other men is when females do this "finger to the dimple" and say, "Well, you know how it is." It is a "babyfying" reaction to a tough situation and sends most men through the roof.

Outsmarting the SeXX Factor
Men really have a hard time in the workplace when they encounter overly-cute, sexy behavior in a woman. While this behavior may get you tickets to the next NBA game, it won't rack up points from men when screenings for promotions are held.

---

4. Verbal Foreplay Belongs at Home
Both Marilou and Judith attend many professional conferences each year. One conference in particular stands out in Marilou's mind.

She observed male and female administrators of similar status working together. They all became quite familiar with one another and developed a spirit of camaraderie, which often is needed in situations that involve hard work and stress. But one woman started to flirt with some of the men in the different groups. She would make sexual references, directing most of her comments at one man in particular. She kept referring to one part of his male anatomy—Big Willy.

The members of the group knew they were just kidding one another and having fun and they openly admitted that watching her mannerisms was exciting. Her behavior, however, caused her Big Willy colleague to respond to her in a typical male-female courting ritual. One male confessed that he had had enough:

> *I get embarrassed when women refer to any part of my anatomy in a playful manner. This type of thing usually happens when I'm in a group of all women. They must feel safe or something. I go along with it. I think,* I'm having fun with this, *but then I realize, my wife would be upset with me.*

As women, we know we can talk to our husbands and boyfriends in this manner. However, at work we only add to men's confusion over whether women should be there and be in positions of power in the first place.

Outsmarting the SeXX Factor

Men are their own worst enemies. They love to "play" with us at work, but feel uncomfortable and uneasy when the "fun" begins. Don't initiate or counter verbal foreplay—it creates a negative opportunity.

---

5. Down and Flirty

Men are attentive to every move a woman makes. How a woman crosses her legs is probably the most noticed behavior and one that sends mixed signals. Brandon is a young corporate executive. He confided that he often feels threatened when a sexy-looking woman comes into his office:

> *I feel somewhat threatened, because she has all the control. All of the props that men use traditionally, the big desk, the decorated office, the big chair, all those things are there to impose authority and control of a situation. Now an attractive woman walks in to do business and crosses her legs...who's in control? She's in control...or thinks she's in control.*

Most of the men interviewed agreed that when women use overly feminine characteristics or gestures at work they often detect these gestures as insincere—phony. Many men perceive these behaviors as a way for the female to step over them to get where they want to go.

No wonder men are confused. For most of them, this is the only way they know how to relate to women. And many women believe they can get whatever they need at work with their sexual edge. Although this may seem like an advantage for them, men resent it.

Harold, a financial executive, revealed his trigger—women who use sex to their advantage, especially when a woman has a position of power within an organization:

> *I hate when women do this, especially the ones in power. It's too distracting and perplexing for me to see a sexy woman or, worse yet, one who's your boss, using her femininity to an extreme. I've seen it in almost every venue.*

And Jon, a stock broker, coat-tailed Harold's comments:

> *Any women who wears a low-cut or semi-open blouse makes it distracting for a man to carry on a conversation.*

Terry is recognized as one of the leading consultants to management. He added:

> *Any woman who wears provocative or see-through clothing ought to expect that men—and women—will stare. If she complains when they do, that would bother me and many others. That being said, in an age of intense sensitivity, let's leave more provocative clothing out of the business world. Such attire has its place, but it isn't in the hallways of commerce.*

Finally, Ken, a successful writer, summarizes his feelings and observations:

> *The only thing that bugs me about women in the workplace is when they intentionally blur the lines of their roles and then get pissed when we get confused. Like, if a woman wore a see-through blouse and then got mad when her subordinates were distracted or started flirting with her. Or, conversely, if she acts like a Nazi guard and then complains that the men around her don't open doors for her. Enough.*

Outsmarting the SeXX Factor

Men love to flirt and are drawn to attractive women. It's a power thing for them—*Hey, I'm in control and she's not.* Don't try to hide your sexiness, rather be aware that flirtatious gestures show a lack of power. When you take that seat in front of him—yes, sit up straight, but don't make a point of sticking your chest out and be circumspect in the way you cross your legs!

Take stock of yourself. Create a mental picture of yourself looking and acting intelligent and successful, making *points with your ideas* rather than your *feminine attributes* to get what you want. The show stopping number from *A Chorus Line*—"Tits and Ass"—belongs on Broadway, not in the office. Using sexual innuendos at work to get your point across is a source for men to feel uncomfortable, anxious and befuddled. You are asking for trouble.

Many women are unaware of their behavior. Develop an awareness of your body movements with men at work. Ask a close, trusted friend to observe you in public. Instruct your friend to notice any overly forward or sensual behaviors you exhibit when you're around men. For women who are very sexual by nature, it is important to control your urge to flirt.

---

6. Keep Your Hands to Yourself—Take the Cue

It's not uncommon for women to continually use subtle sexual cues whenever they relate to men in power. Women may be attempting to make the most of a pressure situation for themselves. And men usually take the bait when offered a hand on the arm or thigh, a tilted head or a nudge on the shoulder. Outside observers, however, are uneasy at this transaction. Trent revealed,

> *I look at the woman as nothing more than a sex object at this point. She knows what she's doing (or maybe not) but one thing's for sure—the guy looks bad. We're at work!*

Some men feel real pain when one of their own makes a fool of himself...and more often than not, it's the woman who shoulders the blame. One male supervisor of a large school district reflected:

> *Women who use their sexiness to get what they want are the very worst in my book. Men are usually helpless. I've learned to manage—*

I am aware of it and know the signs to watch for. I become agitated when I observe a guy getting caught up in this sort of thing. I feel like tipping him off, but then I think—he's an adult and should know what she's up to.

Outsmarting the SeXX Factor

Know that men feel especially uneasy and often confused by your intent with personal, physical touching. Just as important, it's his male friends who feel uncomfortable watching a guy lose his "power" to a woman colleague. Ultimately, it's the woman who loses out. Keep your hands to yourself.

Sandra Grymes and Mary Stanton, in their book, *Coping with the Male Ego in the Workplace,* point out that the problem of misinterpreting body language is alive and well. They tell of a female flight attendant who was offended by the men who often made sexist jokes in front of her. She was sure she never encouraged them to do so. She learned from a sociologist that she had been causing the problem all along. "When women listen to each other or to men, they maintain eye contact for long periods of time, they tilt their heads as if they are hanging on every word and from time to time they smile," he told her. "I used to think that all the women I knew believed I was fascinating and brilliant until I figured out this is the way the majority of women listen." The women's behavior did not mean they were agreeing with everything the sociologist said. Often it just meant they were listening. Nothing more.

7. Geisha Wannabes Not Welcome Here

Along with the woman who acts helpless or cutesy is the woman who caters exclusively to men. We aren't talking about sexual favors; rather, coquettish, submissive behavior *ad nauseam.* In Japan, a geisha is a woman who is trained as an entertainer and to serve as a hired companion to men. She flirts with them and displays physical or verbal affection and submissiveness toward them. In this country, you can find geisha wannabes in almost any organization or neighborhood. Usually, their behavior ends up angering women and men both inside and outside of the workplace.

Martha was very open about the annoyance she felt when the company geisha receptionist was pouring it on:

She had discovered that her key way of getting along with any of the men was to please them and be an outrageous flirt. She would offer to give a neck rub if one of the guys looked stressed, offer to run their personal errands on company time (remember—she's the receptionist, not a personal gofer) and constantly ignore the other women in the workplace.

One day, she came up as a topic at our quarterly meeting. The rest of the women there were relieved to hear that the guys were also uncomfortable with her behavior—it wasn't just us. It was decided that the men would tell her no more neck rubs and running personal errands. Meanwhile, the other women would begin to give her more work that she could do at her desk.

We weren't very successful. She would put off our work if any of the men approached her desk—she would even get up and follow them to the coffee room or their office to see if they needed anything done. She would do anything to engage them in conversations. After a while, they started to complain that she was bugging them! We finally let her go.

Outsmarting the SeXX Factor

Geisha Wannabes need to realize that their paychecks come from the combined revenues created by all employees, not just a few men. This behavior is a negative factor in any workplace or environment. Recognizing that it undermines all work relationships is one way to begin ushering it out. Left to fester, disharmony will increase and relationships can be shattered and promotions lost.

When Marilou and Judith asked the men in their survey whether they were ever distracted by mannerisms that hinted at sexuality, it wasn't uncommon to get a snicker or two. Then they got serious. Did they appreciate attractive women? You bet. Did they want to have fun at work or in activities that both women and men participated in? Yes again. Did they want to have their work or relationships with other women jeopardized because of inappropriate behavior? No. It is important for women to recognize this and eliminate the sexually suggestive behaviors listed if they want to get ahead and stay ahead.

Two women were working on a project with me. One turned out to be a bit on the lazy side, and her lack of performance during a particular job turned out to hurt us in production.

Afterwards, the other woman said to me, "See, I told you she was lazy."

I said, "No you didn't. You never told me that."

To which, she responded, "Well, I was giving you hints."

– Bob, Author and Speaker

6

Yakkity Yak:
Genders Talk, But Do They Listen?

If you ask men what is the most annoying thing about women, many of them often say that women talk too much. It's as simple as that.

In the 1990s, the groundbreaking book, *You Just Don't Understand: Women and Men in Conversation* by Deborah Tannen, topped the bestseller lists for four years. As a linguistics expert, Tannen studied the genders in communication styles for decades. Her miscommunication trilogy includes *Talking from 9 to 5: Women and Men in the Workplace—Language, Sex and Power, That's Not What I Meant: How Conversational Style Makes or Breaks Relationships* and *The Argument Culture: Stopping America's War of Words*. John Gray's *Men Are from Mars, Women Are from Venus,* born in 1992, also climbed the best-seller lists. Communicating was hot. Mis-communicating was big business for the publishing industry.

Most people think of power as having money. For some, that may be true. In reality, power comes in other forms. One of the most powerful tools you will acquire comes from communicating: by being able to speak loudly and clearly so that what you meant to convey is understood and by having the verbal savvy to articulate your words in the right context.

A lack of good communication skills labels people as being less confident, less attractive and less qualified to do a job.

It's the Grapevine, Not Gossip

In programs that Judith oversees on the topic of communicating, she uses her *Are You Communicating?* quiz. Using a true-false format, one of the questions asks if men gossip more than women. The answer is no...but men do gossip—they call it the grapevine.

There is a specific difference in the way the genders communicate. Where women are more inclined to speak and hear as a means of connecting and sharing intimacies, men view communicating as power, status and a measure of independence. Men want information. They use it to create/establish status and display independence. In the grapevine, men could care less what another is wearing, what the setting is or anything that really doesn't relate to the "facts" of the situation. Women, on the other hand, want to hear it all—who was there, what they were wearing, what kinds of feelings were being expressed and facts, too, yes, they're important—but they are just part of the overall "stage."

Men often perceive that women who break from traditional female conversational styles are aggressive. In fact, women also view other women who are outspoken and assertive as too aggressive. When women talk in boastful, assertive and directive patterns, they run the risk of sounding too masculine—and can trigger the SeXX Factor among men in the workplace.

Women are more likely to speak in styles that are less effective in getting recognized and being promoted. If they speak in the styles that are effective when used by men—being assertive, highly confident, talking up what they have done to make sure they get credit for it, jumping in and saying they can do something even though they may be clueless about how to do it—women run the risk of alienating others by not fitting into our culture's expectation of appropriate gender behavior. The serious risk, however, is that women may be ignored or passed over.

Think Hillary Rodham Clinton. Before Bill Clinton ran for President of the United States, she was identified as one of the top 100 lawyers in America. She was outspoken, opinionated and aggressive. In other words, her "style"—communicating and work—alienated men and women. She wasn't what they expected and, in some cases, wanted. Thus, Hillary had a quasi-makeover for the campaign trail—cookie baking was in, speaking out was pushed aside.

Just the Facts, Ma'am

Men think that the female style of indirect communication not only causes confusion and frustration for them, but also is manipulative.

Many women frequently let their sentences dangle: They surround their statements with *I'm not sure, but...* or *You may not agree...* Sometimes this results from low self-esteem, but often it is because women tend to think while they speak. Men's irritation with this stylistic difference can be heard in comments like, *Get to the point!* or *What are you trying to say?*

Many women tend to use indirect styles of communicating when they give feedback to others. Studies also find that women are more indirect about getting others to do things. Ironically, people with direct styles of asking others to do things perceive anyone using indirect requests as manipulative. An example of this is the woman who asks, "Is it too hot in here?" Men would prefer her to ask, "Does anyone mind if I open the window?"

Conversational rituals are used in conversations when you talk without actually thinking about the literal meaning of the word or phrase. For example, a person hearing the question, "How are you?" is not expected to call forth a detailed account of aches and pains. Males and females often have different conversational rituals, which can trigger the SeXX Factor in men who are interacting with women. Apologizing at the drop of a hat is a common trigger for men. Women are frequently told "Don't apologize" or "You always apologize" by male colleagues who view this as synonymous with a putdown of oneself. For women, apologizing can actually be part of an ongoing conversational ritual among women used to restore emotional balance in a conversation. *I'm sorry* can be an expression of understanding—and caring—about the other person's feelings rather than an apology. It's being empathetic. It's also on the list of Behaviors that cause many men to suffer the SeXX Factor.

Which Style Are You?
Here are thirteen different communication styles and rituals that the authors' research has shown create triggers for men. Become aware of those in which you see yourself. You may want to delete them from your communication cache.

1. Bragging Rights...The Art of Self-Promotion
Women don't boast well. Since girlhood, they've had it drilled into them that nice girls don't brag. Get over it—you need to brag. If you don't brag, others will take your accomplishments and claim them for themselves or you will become invisible. However, there's a fine line

between taking credit for the work you do and acknowledging it and outright boasting. When a woman is too audacious, many men think of her as overly competitive and self-focused—something not expected from a female. Therefore, women need to practice what we might term "singing one's own praise" with subtlety.

A male CEO said:

> *I have found the behaviors of some females to be self-aggrandiz-ing or overstatements of their accomplishments. If the example is a good program or a good way of doing things, then put it out there subtly and everyone will know it came from you. But women don't have to overstate their accomplishments. This really irritates men.*

Wendy recently interviewed for a high level position in her organization. She believed she had interviewed extremely well and was confident that her credentials were impeccable. However, she did not land the promotion. Later she asked a female friend who had served on the interview panel her opinion of why she had been passed over. Wendy's friend noted that the screening committee thought Wendy was "too full of herself."

After every question, her friend reported, Wendy would give an example of one of her accomplishments to support the knowledge related to that specific question. Wendy's informer confessed that the applicant who scored the most points with the committee was a young man who presented himself in a well-coordinated package that wasn't only about work. She told Wendy:

> *He carried on at great lengths about his qualifications for the job as well as his former football accomplishments and coaching accolades. He even managed to slip in the "hole-in-one" he got back in 1998.*
> *These events had nothing to do with the interview questions, but the men and women on the screening committee loved him.*

Another male executive confirmed his gender's contempt for the woman who boasts too much at work. "If there is one thing I detest in a woman," he said pointedly, "it's *I talk* rather than *We talk.*"

The problem for most women is that it seems to be difficult to get noticed at work for accomplishments without being perceived as a "braggart." That fine line between bragging and getting lost in the crowd is a difficult one to straddle.

Outsmarting the SeXX Factor

Since it is the perception of competence rather than actual performance that often determines evaluations, learn the subtle skills of self-promotion. Practice how to make a point without coming on too strong. Don't forget that the promotions in corporations often go to those who get the most and best PR.

---

2. In The Fast Lane...She Knows How to Work the Crowd

Women know how to network. Men know that it's important both professionally and socially, but don't always give it a high priority. Watch the women in a large group the next time you're at a conference, convention, trade show, professional meeting or community or social event. Most carry on full conversations with six to eight people in a group in addition to thinking about their next move in the room. Susan RoAne, author of *How to Work a Room*, says, "Women are masters at working the room. They can talk, walk and gather business cards faster than a speeding bullet."

"These kinds of actions leave most men flat-footed," one male manager revealed. Men have remarked that women look too obvious when they "work a room," and women who constantly work the political arena often alienate their male colleagues. That reaction may be one of envy.

One male director described a female colleague's networking needs:

> *I decided to carpool to a Palm Springs work retreat with a woman in our organization since the trip from Los Angeles would take three hours. She was junior to my position and excited about the trip. She planned on using the weekend to meet new people in the organization. She had, however, only one thing on her mind—promotion, promotion, promotion.*
>
> *Traffic was a mess and was at a virtual freeway standstill. Catching a glimpse of her out of the corner of my eye, I could see her literally rocking back and forth. She then began this furious foot tapping. Finally, she couldn't stand it any longer, threw her head into her hands, hitting the dashboard and gasped, "What are we going to do? This traffic is cutting into my networking time."*

Women are aware of the importance of networking in order to break into higher-level positions in their organizations. One thing they may not be aware of, however, is how obvious this may appear to the men observing from the sidelines. They are watching and some of them think that it's way too obvious.

Outsmarting the SeXX Factor

Yes, know how to work the crowd and continue to recognize its importance. But don't be brassy—there's nothing wrong with being skillful and learning the art of being subtle. Be a standout, not towering over the crowd so that you don't connect with those below.

---

3. Too, Too Much...He Likes it Quick and Easy

The woman director stood up in front of the crowd and began to give her report on how she had refined the employee application process for her company. She began with, "On a dark and stormy night when I had nothing to do at home..." and finished one hour later with "Perhaps in the year 2010 no one will ever need to fill out these application forms." The men in the room were beside themselves with agitation and boredom. What should have been a clean ten-minute delivery turned out to be a sixty-minute nightmare for most men in attendance.

John Seymour, a male executive remarked:

> *Who cares that she had nothing to do at home or what the application process may look like in twenty years. Sometimes I think women like to hear the sound of their own voice and fill in the blanks with flowery descriptions and personal stories that have little relevance to the task at hand.*

Outsmarting the SeXX Factor

So what's the big deal? If men want information quick and to the point, then make them happy. If a meeting schedule allots you ten minutes then stick to your ten-minute timeline.

---

4. Is It Hot in Here?...Just Open the Window

You know how it works. We've all seen it and probably ten minutes ago a woman somewhere was heard to say something along these lines:

Is it too hot in here?
Do you think the music is too loud?
Is anyone hungry?
Do you want that last piece of pizza?

Why do women do this? People have different ways of communicating and this indirect style is associated with females 99 percent of the time. Many researchers believe that historically woman have had to use language circumspectly to get what they want. By trying to communicate in a shy, coquettish manner most women think they can get what they want without being perceived as "pushy."

Many women truly believe that only an insensitive, uncouth person would need a direct verbal message. Most men, particularly in the workplace, are confused and frustrated with indirect messages. In addition, the majority of men interviewed perceived that these indirect suggestions were manipulative and weak.

Outsmarting the SeXX Factor

Try these on for size. Practice some of the following:

1. I think it's hot in here. Does anyone mind if I open this window?
2. Please turn down the music.
3. I'm hungry. Let's go to that Chinese restaurant down the street.
4. I'd like the last piece of pizza.

Try it. You'll like it.

---

5. Idle Chatter...She's Thinking Out Loud Again

Call it what you like. Some call it *sub-vocalizing* while others call it *thinking out loud*. It bugs men—they hate it. Women love it. This is how it goes:

Well, first we'll need to get together a committee of people...they must be interested...perhaps we should have three males and three females...no, wait, four females and two males, after all this issue concerns woman and females should be in the majority...then we'll meet in the morning, a breakfast meeting...yes, that would be fun, we'll get to know one another...perhaps we can all say something that happened to us recently that we're particularly proud of...then we can move to the conference room for coffee and handouts...are you running with me on this?

Outsmarting the SeXX Factor

Think about what you want to say ahead of time. Ask a critical friend to spot-check you on your next oral presentation. The goal is to stick to the point, be organized, don't waste time—others and yours.

---

6. Yakkity Yak...He's Lost the Will to Talk

You can't watch a comedy show on television without hearing a joke that makes reference to a woman's excess amount of speech. Women are aware that others think they talk a lot. The truth of this faulty stereotype, however, is that *men* actually do most of the talking, not women. Study after study reports that men talk more at meetings, in mixed group discussions and in classrooms. In groups, men are more inclined to interrupt others than women are. Think about it. Who did your teacher usually call on in school? Yes, it was that boy waving his hand furiously in the air or blurting out the answer, not even waiting to be called on.

What men don't do is talk about feelings and divulge personal information; hence the belief that they talk less. Woman talk about feelings and anything else. The stereotype that women talk more than men does exist in the workplace. Actually, only a few women really drive it home—most women know when enough is enough. Women are expected to talk to a greater extent than men to keep the interaction within a group flowing smoothly, to show goodwill toward others and to talk about matters relevant to personal relationships. Men don't have a problem with that. What they do have a problem with is the woman who won't shut up in meetings or casual conversations. Women who monopolize the floor, won't let anyone speak or who talk nonstop about a subject equally disturb men.

Several men at work reported on their frustration with women who just plain "talk too much." One said:

I think women communicate with too many words. Their kind of "yakkity yak" type of talking is a real turn-off to me.

There are certain female styles of over-talking that cause real irritation in men. "Let's get on with it," they say. "Let's get to the heart of it." The men roll their eyes upward seeming to say, "Enough is enough...so what's the purpose behind this?"

Another executive discussed how a particular woman's over-talking kept her out of the running for a promotion:

So I've got two really worthy candidates; one's a male and one's a female...interestingly enough, the female candidate has some great experience, training and accomplishments. Unfortunately, what will keep her out of the running is her excessive amount of talk, her overdoing and giving every subject more embellishment than necessary and wanting to make sure that everyone understands every detailed piece of information. It's simply not necessary.

Outsmarting the SeXX Factor

Many women love to talk. It is their way of being kind, generous and letting each person know every detail so that everyone is clear and happy. STOP...ABSOLUTELY NO MORE...BY NO MEANS... NO, NO, NO! Of all the behaviors that create the most problems for women, it's over-talking that ranks highest on the SeXX Factor Meter. Talking too much can kill off more chances for promotions to power positions than women could ever hope to know.

Unfortunately, it doesn't matter that even though it is the perception that women talk too much, it is actually the men who do most of the talking. The comedians have had their fun and the chattering female has become a stereotype. Women in power know that most men think women talk too much. If you have the courage, do a reality check and ask a critical friend (preferably a male) if he thinks you talk too much in meetings or conversations. Push hard for an honest answer.

If your friend suggests that yes, you are a bit too talkative... take heed, swallow your pride and change your ways. Use your new awareness to manage your amount of talk by practicing limiting what you say and how you say it. When speaking on a subject to more than a few people, itemize areas on a small note card that you want covered. Don't stray. Try to use fewer words and fewer examples to describe situations. The sheer knowledge that you are prone to excessive amounts of speech usually helps with this process.

7. Flawed Pauses...Did Someone Say "Uhhhh"?
A female director disclosed the following scenario:

> One day I was sitting in a very long meeting and noticed that three of the men in the group were keeping some type of score on their agendas in front of them. All at once the three men made a mark in unison on their scorecards. I was instantly curious. I tried to figure out what they were counting. It didn't take me long and I was appalled. These guys were counting the female coordinator's "uhh-hhs" and "you knows" as she presented her information to the group.
>
> Her speech went on forever (over-talking) and sure enough, every eight to ten words were prefaced with a drawling "uhhhh." My head started to spin. She wouldn't or couldn't stop. What a nasty habit I began to think. I then started to count the "uhhhhs" and "you knows," quickly ticking off twenty-seven before she was cut off by her boss.
>
> After the meeting I went back to my office to locate a recent video recording I had made as a training manual for new employees. As I listened to my ten minute address on the television screen, I counted sixty-five "uhhhs" and twenty-three "you knows." I was hopeful that no one had kept score.

Is this speech pattern exclusive to women? Absolutely not. Men stammer, umming and ahhing and uhhhing just as women do. But, and it's an important but, when you aren't in control or have power, it can work against you. Be aware.

Unfortunately, most people are on automatic pilot when they communicate. Sometimes the brain is not put in gear before the mouth opens. Speech patterns are learned early on and engaged with little thought. Childhood speech characteristics are deeply imprinted by the time a person reaches adulthood. An ingrained speech pattern, whether it is stuttering, littering your speech with "umms" and "ahs" or even slurring words, can damage your credibility and your ability to get a point across

---

Outsmarting the SeXX Factor
If you are caught using excessive "uhhhs" and "you knows" in your speech, work to control this lazy speech habit that definitely drives men (and others) crazy.

---

8. Walk a Mile in His Shoes...It's a Little Thing
When you walk with a man down the hall or to your car after work, do you ever leave him standing on the sidelines after you've run into an old friend or someone you need to talk to? This may sound overly simple, but many men report that this small incident causes them a great amount of frustration. It goes something like this: You meet Steve in the corridor and engage him in casual conversation. You both are on your way to the parking lot and decide to walk out together. You walk with him for a few hundred feet and run into Sue. You stop and talk about some important business. Steve tries to be a "gentleman" and hangs in there with you. You walk on again and meet another colleague. You stop and chat. Steve's patience begins to wear thin. Usually a man won't do this to a woman once he's started walking with her.

As a supervisor, Steve elaborates on this:

> *It's a little thing, but it really drives me crazy when I have to stop and wait while these small discussions take place. I feel like an idiot just standing there. If a woman is going to do this sort of thing, please release me by saying, "You go on, Steve...I'll see you tomorrow."*

Outsmarting the SeXX Factor
Your awareness and avoidance of this trait that frustrates men will gain big points with them in and out of the work environment.

---

9. www.tellawoman.com...The Rumor Mill
Do you remember the old riddle... *What are the three fastest forms of communication? Telegraph, telephone and tell a woman.* What used to be a cute

joke for men isn't so funny for today's women. If you like to gossip you risk losing your chances for promotions to better jobs or higher positions of power in other organizations. Men hate gossip and continually maintain that women who gossip should have no proximity to power in any group setting.

Many men have difficulty trusting others because of the competitive nature of their relationships and often feel that they can only trust themselves. This issue of trust is closely linked to the ritual of gossip in their workplace and their personal spheres. Many men simply will not trust women who gossip and they feel violated when anything about themselves is revealed in this way.

In the past, one avenue to power for women was through gossip. Through gossip, women could control norms, track individual behavior in relation to the norms and build community. Men, on the other hand, disparage gossip and take pride in being discreet. Most men feel women's motivation for gossip is linked with that of retribution. They suggest that women will gossip about people who have irritated them rather than express their anger directly. Men indicate that women who gossip at work are not perceived as very serious people and are often tolerated only for their entertainment value.

Outsmarting the SeXX Factor

Every woman knows that the power of gossip lies in trading on useful information, such as "so and so is going for that promotion," and "so and so got drunk at the office party and is no longer a contender." The trouble with gossip is that men think women who gossip cannot be trusted. While the information contained in the rumor mill can be important for one's career positioning, it's important to distance oneself from the source of the gossip. Listen intently when others reveal office secrets but never comment directly. Better yet, look away and act disinterested, all the while taking in everything you can. Finally, always be aware that information obtained through gossip may not be totally accurate. Also keep this in mind—if you don't want it repeated, don't say it.

---

10. Please Forgive Me...So Sorry

"I am so sorry...I apologize...you may have already thought of this but..."
Count them. On any given day you will never go without hearing one

woman say, "I'm sorry." Most women view "I'm sorry" as something that keeps them on good terms and helps to encourage intimacy with others. Researchers indicate that most women use the apology to establish or restore emotional balance in conversations. Men, on the other hand, perceive the apology as a one-down position and perceive women as weak when they habitually say, "I'm sorry."

When people apologize, it is usually an expression of regret at having done something wrong to another. Unfortunately, women are harder on and more judgmental of themselves when it comes to accepting or taking on blame. Men tend to apologize only when it is expected or when it can't be avoided. In fact, sometimes men never say, "I'm sorry." Instead, they make another statement with the "I'm sorry" implied, as in "I screwed up."

One of the reasons men avoid apologizing is that it tends to put them in an inferior position. Since women are often people pleasers, being apologetic doesn't make them feel put down. According to Deborah Tannen in *You Just Don't Understand*,

> There are many ways in which women talk that make sense and are effective in conversation with other women. When in conversation with men, they appear powerless and self-depreciating. One such pattern is that women seem to apologize all the time.

One thing to keep in mind is that it is not necessary to apologize over a situation in which you have no control. If a land mine is exposed (or explodes), it's sufficient to state whatever the problem is (minus any apologies), followed by recommended solutions to fix it. What Tannen implies is that when the issue is between women, it's okay to apologize; in fact, it can be advantageous in creating a bond and even encouraging intimacy. For men, though, apologizing may be construed as a weakness.

A successful Boston lawyer disclosed:

> It was difficult to break my two young daughters from their tendency to constantly say, "I'm sorry" to just about everything. I didn't notice that they were apologizing so much until I observed this ritual in my own law firm.
>
> On one day, five different female lawyers all offered me a token apology of "I'm sorry." One was for a dropped piece of paper and another was for using too much paper on a memorandum. Another "I'm sorry" was offered for not having a pencil when asked who in the

room had one and still another expression of regret was uttered for a slight interruption in her speech. Finally, an apology from a woman was given for not wearing a watch when asked what time it was. Enough is enough.

Outsmarting the SeXX Factor

This apologetic ritual is hard to break but it can be done with a little bit of practice. Become aware of when, where and the number of times you use "I'm sorry" in any one day.

Create a self-improvement plan to reduce this sorry habit. Try to catch yourself each time you utter an "I'm sorry" and pinch yourself real hard. If you can't break the "I'm sorry" routine, try substituting, "Excuse me…"

This replacement is not half as bad as an apology and takes the curse off your weakened power position. Saying "I'm sorry" every time you try to present important information or apologizing for speaking can be deadly both in the workplace and in your personal life. Once you've become aware that it's a nasty habit… your ability to overcome it will be even easier.

---

11. I'm So Nice…Polite As Can Be

Another factor that appears to have a greater drawback for women than for men is the use of *polite* speech. On one side, it shows a high regard and respect for another. That's not bad. Some cultures covet this behavior. But there are times when too-polite speech lacks the necessary assertiveness or forcefulness.

Sometimes, women feel inhibited to ask for something boldly. So as not to appear too bold, it is common to soften a statement. Let's say you want to go to lunch. Instead of saying, "Let's go to lunch" to a coworker, you might say,

Gosh, I'm famished and I've been so busy; would you like…

Oh, you're probably really busy too, and don't have time to take a break…

Do you think you'd like to get a bite to eat with me…

Because many women are process-oriented in their relationships, they are that way with answers and explanations as well. When someone asks you something, it's not uncommon to tell the reasons in detail of how you arrived at your answer. Some people love to hear all the details; others don't. They'd rather you focus on the bottom-line impact.

Outsmarting the SeXX Factor
Women need to learn goal-oriented language in order to relate their messages more effectively. Otherwise, no one listens.

---

12. Close the Door...Faux Pas That Tag Along
In almost every book on communication, there is mention of women's use of *tag* questions or qualifiers. Whether women use them more than men is not clear. There is a debate. The important fact is for you to be aware of speech mannerisms you use that can be misinterpreted. Typical *tag* questions include—

> *This needs to be completed by four o'clock. Is that okay with you?*

> *We need to be at the meeting at 10:00 A.M. tomorrow. Is that a problem for you?*

Where the first sentence is declarative, the second sentence—the tag—can be interpreted as a window for choice. The receiver of the remark may say, "No, it's not okay with me" or "Yes, it's a problem."

Other factors of nonassertive speech patterns that can get you into trouble include the use of *qualifiers*. Qualifiers are often interpreted as a form of discounting what is being said. Qualifiers are hedges—words or phrases that make you sound uncertain—

> *You know...*
> *Sorta...*
> *I guess...*
> *I suppose...*

When you are uncertain, *qualifiers* are perfectly legitimate. But as fillers or hedges, they *lessen your power* when communicating with another. Examples of beginning sentence phrases are—

I'm not sure that this is a good idea, but...

You may think this is dumb (stupid, silly, idiotic)...

Women also get into trouble when they use too many adverbs or adjectives. The result is that their speech is sometimes trivialized. Examples are "It's so lovely and wonderful to be here today" and "I think this is so very wonderful, exciting and fabulous. I know it's going to be beyond belief."

Another common speech faux pas is inviting disagreement. When you have a strong opinion about a situation or you require someone's participation, it doesn't make sense to preface your statement or request with a disclaimer—

I may be wrong, but...

You may not like what I'm going to say, but...

Outsmarting the SeXX Factor

Not only do such statements and phrases lessen your speech and presence power, they also invite your listeners to move into a defensive posture and disagree with you even before you have a chance to make a statement. Being friendly can do wonders in the right place at the right time, but it also can be a distraction. Practice strengthening your speech by eliminating qualifiers and excessive descriptive words.

---

13. It's Not What You Say...It's What Is Seen

Unassertive-type mannerisms like not making eye contact or smiling inappropriately, get women into trouble. As a rule, women are more inclined to create eye contact with the person they are talking to. That's the good news; don't avoid it. Good eye contact is a communications gesture that should be mastered early on. With it, you are more likely to be taken seriously. If your eyes constantly hop around, rarely connecting with the person you are talking to, your remarks can easily be interpreted as meaning you're not serious or you're nervous. As a result, a subtle message can be sent that your concern, opinion or statement is not important.

In addition to using speech patterns that are unassertive, women are far more likely to smile inappropriately, especially during times of conflict, than are men. It is not uncommon for both men and other women to interpret a smile during a stressful or conflicting time to mean that all is okay, you're okay, and the issue is not as big a deal as you feel it is. It is also not uncommon, during stressful and painful times, for women to laugh or, worse, giggle.

Robert is a real estate broker. His take on a recent sales meeting:

> We have weekly sales meetings in our office. Brenda is one of the newer agents and has done quite well. At the meeting last week, a dicey situation came up where one of the other agents had shown property to one of Brenda's clients and then made an offer.
>
> If this had happened to me, I'd be pissed. Brenda was fairly quiet, even smiling. We all thought that there must be some agreement with the two agents to share the client or commission. It turned out there wasn't. Brenda blew up after the meeting, even threatening to quit if the manager didn't remove the other agent. But her behavior during the meeting seemed to indicate she had no problem with the other agent's actions. It was confusing.

Do you remember when Anita Hill testified at the Senate hearings in the mid-nineties, before Clarence Thomas was affirmed as a justice of the Supreme Court? During those hearings, when various questions, innuendoes and even accusations were directed toward Hill from the committee members, it was not uncommon to see her nodding slightly or bobbing her head. That type of mannerism sends off confusing signals. It almost seemed as if she were agreeing with them.

Normally, when listeners nod their head up and down, most people assume that they agree with the speaker. Not necessarily so. Women appear to be more inclined to nod their heads during a conversation than do men—even though they don't agree with what's being said. It's more of a mannerism of taking information in. During the Thomas hearings, the thoughts in Anita Hill's head were probably more along the lines of: *These senators sound like bozos.* Head bobbing and nodding can make you appear submissive or that you are in agreement with someone, when you actually aren't.

Outsmarting the SeXX Factor

It is imperative to understand that most communication is nonverbal, with the majority coming from gestures, inflections and body language. If you give off "false" communication—inappropriate smiling, giggling or body language, your message is misinterpreted and you lose your credibility.

What is the bottom line when it comes to communication? First, moving beyond miscommunication, non-communication and wrong communication is critical. Second, by not communicating a problem when it occurs, your silence tells the other person it's okay to continue doing whatever is being done—that no change is necessary. And third, neither men nor women are the "better" communicators. Both women and men must learn to be more flexible in their styles of speaking as well as in their interpretations and understanding of speaking. It is unwise to ignore the fact that there are communication differences between genders as well as cultures.

Your ability to be assertive is the basis of clear and honest communication between you and others. Most communications and behaviors fall into three categories: assertive, passive/submissive (nonassertive) and aggressive. Aggressive behaviors can be divided into direct and indirect.

Women who are nonassertive are most likely reluctant or unable to confidently say and express what they feel, believe or think. When you cross the line from assertiveness—confidently expressing yourself—to outright aggression, you enter troubled waters. There's a big difference. Granted, you are expressing yourself, but with aggressive behavior the method in which you are doing it often involves intimidating, degrading or even demeaning another person.

By speaking directly, succinctly, with forethought and assertively—not aggressively—and encouraging others to do the same, you will significantly reduce miscommunication, non-communication and wrong communication in both your workplace and your personal life.

Shortly after Whoopi Goldberg hosted the Academy Awards, she appeared on the Tonight Show *with Jay Leno. There had been a lot of negative chatter in the media about her hosting skills and even about her outfits and hairstyles at the Awards show. Leno brought this up in his interview, mentioning that none of the criticisms were attributed to anyone in particular. Whoopi's response? "People who stab you anonymously aren't real people."*

And so it goes with the gossip pool...especially when they hide behind one another.

7

Barracudas, Bullies and Broads: Fact or Fiction?

Men do it and women do it, but men and women generally do it differently. Most often, if a man is a saboteur, gender is not an issue; the target can be either sex. But women are more inclined to undermine and sabotage their own gender. This activates the SeXX Factor, as well.

Did you know that the word sabotage is derived from the French word, *sabot*, which is a wooden shoe? The act of sabotage was identified when French machinists protested working conditions by throwing their shoes—their sabots—into the machines to stop work.

This action resulted in severe damage to whatever equipment was the target of one's footwear. Today, men and women don't take their shoes off and throw them into machinery, but the damage done by any sabotage can be just as effective. Mayhem, destruction, betrayal, treachery and seduction are all associated with it.

What is the Sabotage Factor?

The undermining or destruction of personal/professional integrity; malicious subversion resulting in damage to personal/professional credibility. The end result is the erosion or destruction of the victim's self-esteem and confidence. Sabotage can be intentional or unintentional and can be delivered overt or covertly.

Since the mid-eighties, Judith has conducted nationwide studies and research on the topics of women, sabotage and bullying in the workplace. The results of the first study were released with the publication of *Woman to Woman: From Sabotage to Support* in 1987. According to the survey, 53 percent of the women surveyed said they had been undermined by another woman, while 63 percent of the women responded they had been undermined by a man.

During the 1990s, significant changes were noted. A slight decrease in men undermining women was reported by the women, but more significantly, a greater number of women were reporting undermining and bullying behavior from other women. A 1994 study showed that sabotage—woman to woman—was the third greatest problem women were experiencing in their workplaces. In fact, sabotage almost tied for second with communication problems.

In 1999, a study undertaken by Judith for *Woman to Woman 2000: Becoming Sabotage Savvy in the New Millennium* reported another increase from the original study, with 75 percent of the women stating that they had been undermined by another woman. And in 2002, Judith conducted a study that exclusively looked at the health care workplace, which is female dominated (*Zapping Conflict in the Health Care Workplace*). More than 80 percent of the nurses reported being undermined or bullied by a manager or coworker and 45 percent had quit their jobs because of it.

Judith also found that men and women differed in their sabotage methodology and style. Men were inclined to be more assertive, direct and overt when they engaged in any type of sabotage. Women, on the other hand, were more inclined to be covert and indirect when sabotaging another person.

Men say they are amazed at the way women undermine other women. Where the men are bold and up front, sabotaging women are more likely to stay behind the scenes. Front-stabbing vs. back-stabbing.

Just Office Politics?

Prior to a recent speaking engagement in New England, Judith did radio and television PR to publicize the event. One of the television segments was to be aired on the five o'clock news. At the television station, after being introduced to the anchor, who was serving also as the reporter for the segment, a series of questions was asked—actually, stated—referencing sabotage in the workplace. In fact, it was the only thing the anchor wanted to talk about, even though presentations were scheduled on three areas, Confidence, Personal Finance and Women and Sabotage in the Workplace.

The reporter's position was that sabotage was normal, basically just office politics. Judith responded, no—undermining and bullying another person goes beyond office politics. There are differences between the way women do it versus men. Also, women tend to over-personalize and react in a more personal way when it happens. The end result is that no matter what, when sabotage occurs, productivity, morale, loyalty, even company profitability are impacted.

Well, the interviewer wasn't interested in talking about crises and their impact on one's personal life, how to rebuild confidence or personal money strategies. It was "sabotage—office politics," or nothing. After leaving the station, Judith learned that this same anchor had recently been suspended from the station for two weeks for harassing a younger female reporter. She had written letters to the reporter stating that the young woman was dumb, that she didn't know how to be a newsperson, that she never looked right, that she didn't know how to speak and that she was too big-breasted.

Outsmarting the SeXX Factor

Create and Maintain Allies. You might be thinking: *It isn't enough I have to deal with men in the workplace, but those "aggressive" women, too.* Remember there is always safety in numbers. Find allies who are coworkers, colleagues, supervisors and managers within the organization. It usually pays to be pleasant toward those in a superior position. To get to where they are, they already have mastered the techniques that allow them to be "Artful Dodgers" of saboteurs. This camaraderie also enables you to allow a supervisor or manager, including those who don't manage you directly, to learn about your accomplishments and achievements.

Don't confuse friendship with friendliness. Allies are the ones with whom you build strong and supportive workplace relationships. They are not necessarily those to whom you open up and share your personal life. When you have strong allies, it is difficult for someone with saboteur and shark tendencies to attack you. Your coworkers will be as tuned in to sabotage techniques as you are and can sound off warnings as well as head off any attacks.

The Bully on the Street...or in the Hallway

The most common reasons why women undermine other women are that they are jealous and lack confidence in their own abilities and self-esteem. They may be fearful that someone is after their job. Saboteurs are, in effect, bullies. Bullies are masters at determining who has less power than themselves. A bully/saboteur attempts to gain power by putting others down. It is much easier to win—to put someone down—when the target has less power and less confidence than the perpetrator, the saboteur.

Since only six million of the fifty-eight million women who work are in management positions, it is fairly safe to assume that if a women has any positional power in the workplace, that power will most likely be over other women. Following that reasoning, if a woman attempts to dis-empower another, the target of her action will most likely be a another woman.

Sabotage weighs heavily in the personal cost arena. Embarrassment, emotional duress and loss of reputation, self-esteem, jobs, promotions and money all rank high as repercussions when women talk about being undermined by another woman.

Women report that society in general *expects* men to display inappropriate, non-supporting and undermining relationships in the workplace. It is almost stereotypical. So, if men do it, what is the big deal when one woman does it to another woman? The answer lies in stereotypes and upbringing—that is, women are supposed to be nice, to be friends, to take turns, to be caring, not to fight, etc., etc. Thus, when they do it, it's a big deal.

The reality is, not only are there a lot of jerks out there, there are "jerkettes." There are men and women with whom you have no business sharing your hopes, your concerns, your fears and your dreams. Women are more inclined to be too open with another and do it too soon—sharing information that a potential saboteur or jerkette, who may not have your best interests in mind, can use against you. Information that you have freely given can and very often will be used against you in personal and work relationships with men and women, as well as within your over-all workplace environment among coworkers and management.

When someone undermines another, the saboteur seeks to gain something, while the victim, in turn, loses something. The gains that most saboteurs make are reputation, promotions, jobs and enhanced self-esteem. These come at the expense of the individuals who were sabotaged. Guess who also loses? The employers. The company can lose in loyalty, productivity, reputation, credibility, team growth and effectiveness. All are fallout factors that affect the bottom line.

Why Do Women Undermine Women?
Women who choose to undermine other women are affected by certain social, cultural, demographic and psychological factors. In Judith's ongoing work, she has pinpointed fourteen major reasons why women are inclined to undermine other women. They are:

- Competition among women in the workplace is greater today. This is due to both demographic and social trends. Women struggle harder to obtain their positions and get ahead, many being the primary source of income for the households.

- The pay disparity between men and women for equal jobs grows. Until women stand together and say, "I won't work unless I get paid what others get paid for the same job," and employers stop playing games and pay everyone who has the same credentials, skills and position equally, pay inequities will continue to be a dominant factor.

- Whenever there is a downturn in the economy, women are pitted against other women when it comes to layoffs. As a rule, if women are in management, they are most likely to be employed in middle- to lower-management. When layoffs and terminations are called for, women are often the first to go.

- Presentday societies continue to experience crises of unethical behavior. Traditional morals and values have declined. This impact seems to be greater on women, since they have traditionally held the family together, setting the tone for its values, its ethics and its morals.

- The workplace is still a jungle. Players struggle to take advantage of various opportunities and to form alliances and cliques with one another. One of the classic examples of this is currently being displayed routinely on the *Survivor* television series that millions tune into each week.

- Women are more likely to be practitioners of participative management style. Their personal style works successfully at times, and, at other times, can backfire because of its greater personal interaction with coworkers and employees.

- If criticism, discipline or reprimands are warranted in a specific situation, a woman may feel betrayed because there was a perceived personal relationship with the manager or supervisor. Women are more likely to develop personal relationships with other women in the workplace; men don't view personal relationships as a priority in their workplace.

- Women are stressed out and overloaded. Extra pressures mount from balancing their family and workplace responsibilities as well as their personal lives. Women's concerns reach out to relationships, pleasing, making wrong decisions, health and healthcare, children, lack of time, aging, parents, job performance, even world affairs. Men often are far more myopic in their concerns.

- Women are still held back from positions they are both capable and qualified to hold. Studies from the Center for Creative Leadership show that Caucasian women have to be three times as knowledgeable and expert to be perceived equal to Caucasian men. Women of color have to be six times more knowledgeable and expert than Caucasian men. Because of such businesses ignorance, women's ability to advance as well as to enhance their income becomes limited.

- Upbringing is always a factor. Women have been raised differently from men and they bring a more flexible and situational approach to relating the world to the workplace. These approaches and methods are consistently passed on to the next generation. Women are more split on their psychological realities. Each gender relates to the world differently and so each has different ideas about what is dishonest and deceptive or competitive, as well as what value they place on self-esteem and relationships. Men deal differently with their feelings of anger and hostility.

- Women are acknowledging that they have been undermined by other women. In the past, women ignored it, didn't talk about it or denied that another woman had displayed sabotaging behavior toward them or others. If a woman spoke up and spoke out, she could be misinterpreted as not supporting other women.

- In order to resolve the problem of women undermining and sabotaging other women and turn it into women supporting women, it is important to understand the genesis of the problem. It doesn't begin in the workplace. No, it seeds from earlier childhood experiences, stereotypes of women and men and the overall psychological makeup of women.

- With an expansion of knowledge, ongoing solutions will be developed and identified to create the changes women need to succeed in the workplace and with themselves. In order to do this, women must realize that not all women behave equally. Nor do all women have other women's best interests in mind—and won't support them.

- Women are reluctant to confront abusive or harassing behavior when it occurs. Because of women's tendencies to remain silent and not speak up and out when behaviors are inappropriate, their silence is often interpreted as an approval or, at least, *no big deal.*

- Gender stereotypes of expected male and female behaviors are continually affirmed and passed on from generation to generation. The end result is that it is difficult to change the old ways and assumptions. The status quo remains.

Are Women Really Barracudas?

The most common form of sabotage is gossip—no special skills or tools are needed. Just how prevalent is gossip in the workplace? The old adage, "Sticks and stones can break your bones, but names can never hurt you," is a myth. Words do hurt. When passed on irresponsibly, whether or not the validity is verified, it is almost impossible to undo the damage. Reputations are ruined, credibility lost and relationships shredded.

Peter works in a Fortune 100 company in Continuing Educational Services in the Pacific Northwest. His group provides industry and business training. He believes it is important to cut through not only the stereotypes of both men and women in the workplace, but to get through all the game playing that goes on.

Peter is a male administrator in a female-dominated group who was brought in from the outside. In the beginning, he found there was a great deal of jealousy among the female workers. Grumbling surfaced over the fact that the position should have been filled from within the existing group. Peter believes that, no matter what, there is always going to be talk about someone, somewhere and he is amazed at the level to which women get involved in the gossiping maze. He believes that if you don't get sucked into the whirlwind of gossip and rumors that can be prevalent in workplaces, schools and other venues, others will begin to judge you on your actual merits. Says Peter:

> *A lot of jealousies happen, especially when you are new on the job. There must have been umpteen numbers of rumors because of the friendships I'd had with several of the women, all platonic. When it comes down to competing in job situations, rumors tend to surface. Recently, I recommended one member of my team for a promotion. Rumors like, "I know how she got the job," began to fly. You would think, in this day and age, we would be beyond that.*
>
> *I worked in team situations with these people and, finally, some said to me, "I know about some of those rumors that have surfaced in the past, but, you know, you are very capable at what you are doing!" It's like, an "Aha moment" and they finally see the light.*

Outsmarting the SeXX Factor

Rumors and gossip don't belong in any sphere of a person's life. They can destroy and alter relationships and careers permanently. Men consistently complain that women gossip too much and view it as senseless chatter. Before passing on any rumors or gossip, determine if it's accurate. If it's not, stop. If it is, ask what purpose there is to continue talking about it. Spreading rumors and gossiping for "the fun of it" will only discount you in other's eyes.

Saboteurs in Your Midst

Sometimes the messengers of sabotage are subtle. Below is a questionnaire to help identify a *Saboteur in the Midst*. They are questions you can ask yourself to assist in uncovering someone who may be setting you up or who is actively involved in some type of sabotage perpetration. A *yes* to any of the questions demands that you be on the alert.

Is There A Saboteur in Your Midst?

1. *Does anyone around you encourage gossip?*
Most saboteurs are messengers—they can hardly wait to pass along damaging information about anyone or anything.

2. *Does anyone keep a tally sheet?*
Everyone makes mistakes—saboteurs usually keep count and can make a big brouhaha out of any small incident.

3. *Does information ever pass you by?*
A common strategy of a saboteur is to isolate others. The most common practice is to withhold information or interrupt the information pipeline/grapevine that could be relevant to your work and other activities.

4. *Does anyone feel her or his job is in jeopardy?*
Whenever there is fear and anxiety resulting from, for example, downsizing, upsizing and reorganization, many people overreact. For some, paranoia sets in.

5. *Does anyone stand to profit by another's mistake?*
Any time someone makes a mistake, saboteurs relish that error; they will be players in the pass-along of the "error" and, because of another's mistake, may eventually benefit by a promotion or bonus, or at the very least, an enhanced reputation.

6. *Have new coalitions formed on your team?*
It is commonplace for saboteurs to continually realign their "friend-ships." With each new realignment, they are often in the center, simi-lar to what happens within a high school clique.

7. *Is anyone on your team sometimes too helpful?*
Until you really know how a group or team operates, an overly help-ful/zealous player may not be what you think she is.

8. *Does anyone routinely deny involvement in activities, yet know all the details?*
Saboteurs are masters at working the grapevine; they are also chameleons. They initially claim no knowledge of any specific inci-dent, yet somehow are able to pass along the details and information to anyone who asks, and, in some cases, doesn't ask.

9. *Does anyone encourage others to take on tasks that appear impossible?*
When you or another person fail at a task, those who are saboteurs take great pleasure in it. The end result is that the failure makes them look good and even savvier for not taking on the impossible.

10. *Does anyone bypass your authority and go over your head?*
Saboteurs will do almost anything to look good, including sidestep-ping a leader's authority or ignoring other team members' contribu-tions.

11. *Does anyone routinely take credit or discount your workplace contribu-tions or other coworkers' contributions?*
Saboteurs rarely compliment or give credit openly for another's work. Their style is more likely to discount participation by other team mem-bers or take credit for themselves. Women are more inclined not to speak up or out when someone hogs the limelight and/or takes credit for another's work.

Source: *Woman to Woman 2000* © 1999 by Judith Briles. All Rights Reserved.

After identifying possible or probable saboteurs, your next step is to deal with them. There are two things that need to come into play. The first is to document, the second is to develop good confronting skills. When you do confront, you need the facts to back up whatever your accusations are. Most saboteurs will do just about anything to avoid any public exposure. They will rarely commit anything to paper, so you will need to have the facts.

Once a saboteur is identified, it is important to sidestep her or his games. Being a saboteur takes a lot of time and commitment. Over time, she—or he—will be less productive. The longer the game goes on, the less the saboteur produces and the more likely that individual is to be exposed to others. The jig is eventually up. Until that happens, the workplace may feel like a battlefield.

Outsmarting the SeXX Factor

Speak-up and Speak-out. In other words, confront the saboteur. The single most important thing to do after you've been sabotaged, is to confront the saboteur. Rarely is this fun, but nevertheless, it is critical so that you can move on. Most women have not been encouraged to engage in conflicts as men have in their formative years.

If you don't confront, you are setting into play a series of factors that will enable the situation to perpetuate. When you don't confront, your message is "Okay, keep doing it." And you might as well add, "Keep doing it to others." Because women are more inclined to internalize anger, it can be re-expressed in a variety of unhealthy ways, some of which can make you quite ill.

Shark Attacks

When women have been undermined by a colleague, coworker or friend, especially if it's another woman, they say it is like being attacked by a snake. It's a quick, brutal strike, sometimes leaving the victim not knowing what hit her. It can seem like swimming in a vast, beautiful sea, where everything seems quiet and peaceful in the waters of life, and then, all of a sudden, along comes a shark and you are bitten. Sabotage and women undermining women will continue to grow unless women stand up and speak out when situations occur.

Scientists estimate one's chances of being bitten by a shark are ten million to one. Your odds of encountering a shark in your workplace or personal life are far greater. With the continued reorganization and downsizing of companies the nineties introduced, your odds are even more enhanced. Women who undermine women—the sharks—are far less likely to undermine those who speak up for themselves and their rights and who display confidence—those who swim assertively. Sharks reason that when there are so many fish in the sea, why waste time on one who could possibly bite back, which is what you must be prepared to do.

When Judith first started writing about sabotage in the workplace, it was not uncommon for her to get letters and telephone calls from women from various parts of the country. Story after story would unfold, some so ludicrous that you couldn't believe that someone could be so caught up or so naive. Others were so painful that she wished she could reach across the telephone lines and hug the caller, giving support and caring as well as shelter from any additional onslaughts.

What she thought would be the solution to the problem with the publication of her first book turned out to be merely the tip of the iceberg. Greater numbers of women are reporting bullying and sabotaging experiences created by other women within and outside of their workplaces. The good news is that other researchers and writers have joined Judith to bring attention to the issue and women are now more aware of this problem.

Outsmarting the SeXX Factor

The last thing you want to do is plot revenge or malign a friend, coworker, boss or company. It ends up being self-destructive and can almost guarantee a visit to the unemployment lines. You may end up being labeled a malcontent or even deserving of your fate. Your model should definitely **not be,** "Don't get mad, just get even."

A healthier approach would be to reframe whatever the situation was and determine what kind of learning experience you can receive from it. In the end, many saboteurs' successes are not as sweet as they envisioned. The deceit and sabotage that enabled them to win an early victory, in the end, may block them from a goal that they sought in the long run. The old adage, "United we stand, divided we fall," definitely applies to women and their sabotaging actions directed toward other women.

I can sense it every time I'm with her... her lack of self-confidence and the doubts she harbors about herself. I keep telling her that she's the best thing we've ever seen in this charitable foundation but she doesn't believe me. She works till midnight, does the huge projects and never says no to anyone's request. What's more, she's intelligent. A lot of the guys in this place are beginning to resent her. I've told her that she needs to loosen up a bit.

– Marvin, Senior Accountant

8

Confidence Crisis:
Women Have It All—Almost

The first decade of the new millennium has generated incredible scenarios and memories around the world, starting with Y2K, the botched Presidential election and September 11, 2001.

Your ability to confront, deal with and grow through events that you sometimes don't create or control, comes into play. *It's called having confidence*—a critical ingredient in moving through and on from events that aren't to your choosing or liking.

In the two national surveys that Judith conducted on confidence, a shift occurred from the first in 1990 and the second in 2001, reported in *The Confidence Factor—Cosmic Gooses Lay Golden Eggs*. Thousands of men and women responded to the question, "Where does confidence come from?" In the nineties, men were more inclined to say confidence comes from "upbringing" (46 percent), while women were more inclined to say "experience" (43 percent). With the turn of the century, over 50 percent of the men AND women reported that "experience" was the key factor (54 percent men and 52 percent of the women stating so). "Upbringing" now trails behind, with 26 percent of women reporting so; more men than women stated that "upbringing" was key at 35 percent, a reversal of the two since the beginning of the nineties.

So, what does this mean? Plenty...the workplace is changing; the stock market ended the decade with a roar and has been topsy-turvy ever since; the Internet promises a whole new way of doing business;

and instead of workaholics, a new way of working has emerged. Generation Y, the Millenniums, say: "Not me. I want a life."

Today, we are older and, hopefully, wiser. Times have changed. It *is* a different workplace and workforce. It's a different population and a different lifestyle. And it's a different attitude than that of the previous decade. Both men and women report that confidence comes from experience. Unfortunately, though women have experience, they still are haunted by demons that erode their confidence.

In the July 22, 2002 issue of *Business Week*, an article titled, "She's Gotta Have 'It'," focuses on confidence…or the lack of it, that continues to hold women back from advancements. "It" is executive presence and refers to the ability to create a polished presence when entering a room, connecting quickly and staying visible. When women with presence speak, others listen. Confident women inspire at all levels—from the CEO to the receptionist. They speak with conviction, never equivocating.

Where are you in the scheme of things when it comes to confidence—highly confident, scraping the barrel or in between? *The Confidence Quiz* below will take you only a few minutes to complete. Use it as an assessment to help you in understanding where you are and where you need to build yourself up—to get that "It" factor.

The Confidence Quiz

As you read each question, write the number in the blank that best reflects how you are thinking and feeling *today* . . .not how you felt *last* week or how you speculate things may be *next* week. It's for *now* and will become part of your guide through the confidence maze of life.

Rarely Or Never	Not Very Often	Occasionally	Frequently	Yes! Most or All of the Time
1	2	3	4	5

_____ Do you enjoy and thrive in the work you do?

_____ Do you acknowledge and take credit for your own accomplishments?

_____ Do you seek out and enjoy learning new things?

_____ Do you limit (or eliminate) your time spent with negative people?

_____ Do you surround yourself with people you admire?

_____ Are you able to ask for something when you need or want it?

_____ When someone criticizes or rejects you, do you assess it, then move on?

_____ When you have failed at something, do you maintain your visibility and stay around others?

_____ Do you forgive yourself for mistakes that you make?

_____ Are you self-reliant, asking, doing and getting things for yourself?

_____ Do you feel that your life is in sync—balanced between work and play?

_____ When you feel strongly (or not so strongly) about an issue or matter, can, and do you express your opinion?

Scoring:

The maximum score you can have is 60 if you scored a 5 on everything, which is unlikely. One of the great secrets that highly confident women and men share is that there are times that they don't feel highly confident. In fact, there are times that they feel that confidence totally eludes them. Surprised? You shouldn't be.

55-60   Extremely Confident—You are a confident woman or man. You've learned how to get, keep and grow your confidence. Bravo!

49-54   Frequently Confident—You have a great deal of confidence and can gain more with just a bit of fine-tuning. More than likely, you are a leader where you work and definitely have the key ingredients to move to the top.

43-48   So-So Confident—You're average, which yields you an average or so-so return in what you do. Why not stretch yourself and learn something new? Review your past accomplishments. It's time for you to get a few accolades, even if you are the only one applauding.

37-42   Not So Confident—Your confidence is shaky. It's time for you to step back and do some probing. Ask yourself, "Am I 'on track' for me?" and "Am I self-reliant, asking and getting things for myself?" It's probable that others control you, with your permission. You need to trust yourself and follow your passions, not others'.

Below 36   Rarely Confident—Yikes...surgery is in order! You need to surround yourself with some plus points...at work and at home. If friends and family are dragging you down, tell them you need some positive support, not negative criticism. Treat yourself to something new. Read a great book; attend a stimulating lecture; see a fun movie. Make a conscious effort to reach out. Aspire higher!

Focus on questions for which you scored less than 3. These reflect where you are today and what's impacted you in the past, as well as what you need to do tomorrow to make positive changes in your life.

Source: © 2001 *The Confidence Factor* by Judith Briles. All Rights Reserved.

Self-esteem and confidence go hand-in-hand. Self-esteem is the regard, appreciation and caring that you have for yourself.
    Confidence takes it further. Confidence is the POWER to replenish and maintain that respect, appreciation and regard you have for yourself.

Bluffing It—The Great Imposter

Many of the women interviewed revealed that they were fearful that a mistake, even an indiscretion from their past, would come back to haunt them. In a focus group in southern California, several high-ranking corporate executives spoke about their fears of being "found out" about their lack of self-confidence. Gail shared:

> *At age twenty-one, I secured my first job as a junior accountant. I never called in sick for the first two years of work. I was literally afraid that my supervisor would somehow find out that I didn't know what I was doing. I have told this story to many women who respond with their own stories. Most women disclosed that they have been fearful at some time in their career that "someone will find out."*

Lisa opened up about the fear that surfaced when she stepped into a new position:

> *I secured a job as the director of marketing after one year as an assistant. I spoke to my friend, a veteran in the field, and complained, "I can't do this...I don't know how to do this." She laughed and informed*

me that most women are wracked with doubt, panic, confusion and anxiety after they gain positions once dominated by males. "Self-confidence," she explained, "is the key. Have confidence in yourself, act like you know what you are doing and soon you will believe it yourself."

Caitlin spoke about her need to prove herself in every task she undertook. The end result was that she either intimidated the men or pissed them off. Her words:

I have a propensity for overdoing everything at work. If I want to have a brunch for management I have a BRUNCH FOR MANAGEMENT. This is no ordinary brunch. I create a theme, start it off with an icebreaker, add in a few funky favors and a PowerPoint presentation on the side. What does this do to men? It de-motivates and ticks them off—they look at that and say, "I can never compete with Martha Stewart."

When speaking to Judith, Caitlin referred to her need to prove or affirm herself as the "Impostor Phenomenon." She continued:

I think we need to look at what scares the pants off the men. Some females are driven by the fact that we're afraid men are going to find out that we can't do this job. So we will do it and everything around it well—they will never be able to find that out. When we can understand that, look at it, come to terms with it and have confidence that we can do the job then we can step back a little... and stop striving to be so damn powerful and perfect. As we gain in power and authority, we exaggerate our sense of power and authority and push other people out.

Outsmarting the SeXX Factor

Men don't even try to do the amount of juggling that women do routinely. Ask yourself how many successes you need before believing you're "the real thing."

Let It Go...She Likes the Last Word

Have you ever been cornered by a dog that won't stop barking at you, no matter how hard you try to make it stop? Men interviewed confess that there's nothing that makes them angrier than women who continue to persevere against them in confrontational situations.

Robert, an executive with a telecommunications company, said:

> *It's the "bulldog" effect. A man and woman get into a disagreement over an issue and they argue their points. No one is winning; it's a standstill. One thing, however, is different for the woman. She won't give up. She continues to drive her point home until the man gives up or leaves the room. I've seen this a hundred times over.*

Jennifer has worked in software development for years. She concurred, adding that she has created the scenario that Robert referred to:

> *I was guilty of driving the point home myself...I was embarrassed that I could take an issue so far. I had the right answer and knew that I was right. The male just didn't get it. I gave him a double dose of all that I had and he broke down and agreed with me. Or was it a concession? It was not a pretty sight. I won. He lost. In retrospect, I think I lost too.*

Outsmarting the SeXX Factor

Take notice when you are involved in a confrontational situation with a man at work. Ask yourself how far you are willing to go to make a point. Take a status check of the level of his anger and frustration and gauge yourself accordingly.

Dirty Pool..."Gotcha"

Some females love to compete with the men in their organization. One CEO discussed situations in which he has observed females who displayed aggressive behaviors in order to affirm their power positions:

> *One female did a "Gotcha" to a male peer in the presence of his colleagues and immediate supervisor. There was this flash of anger from the male. I recall the female's smug satisfaction that she had shared something that had gone wrong for this man in the company of others.*

Richard, a manufacturing director, remarked about women who he feels are too passive aggressive:

> *When a woman gets mad at something that one of the guys has done in this office, she usually doesn't deal with it right away. It's*

like she saves it up and gets the guy later, say in a meeting or in front of his friends.

Outsmarting the SeXX Factor

Don't play games at work. If there's a problem, identify the issues and deal with it…directly with the other party vs. grandstanding it in front of others. Don't play dirty pool with men at work. It's a myth that if you make someone else look foolish, you will look better.

A Matter of Insult…May the Best (Wo)Man Win

Men relish the art of ritual opposition. It's part of their persona. Women don't—they hate it and feel that to banter back and forth with one another just for fun or because it feels good is a waste of time, an insult or just plain stupid. Men derive great sport from a good argument and find pleasure in the ritual nature of verbal opposition. Women don't. We often take the challenges as personal attacks and find it impossible to do our best in a contentious environment.

Women commonly mistake the art of ritual opposition with a male as a personal attack against them. When a woman senses that she has played all her cards in what a male finds a natural verbal exchange, the game—and it is a game—shifts. Her arsenal of goodies comes out. This may include insults, snippy tones in her voice or laying out guilt trips.

Paul, a senior vice president, commented about women's aversion to ritual opposition:

> *In a meeting, when two men disagree over an issue, it's common for them to go back and forth, each raising what they believe to be the finer points of the argument. This seems very natural for men.*
>
> *When women do it, however, they seem uncomfortable. They take every word to heart as if it's a personal attack against them. They often get mad at the other person and start plotting the pay backs.*

Outsmarting the SeXX Factor

Disagree with dignity and let the best wo(man) win. Catch yourself when you begin to sense that you are involved in a verbal exchange that resembles ritual opposition. Know that he likes to bat the ball into your court and eagerly waits for your volley. Be kind.

The Winner's Circle...In Your Face

Men think that some women, in their attempt to conquer their lack of self-confidence, try to overcompensate by acting overly confident in the workplace. Steven works within the insurance industry. His take:

> *I have seen women try to overstate their expertise about a certain issue...or to prove a point, continue to use "in your face" type of behavior with men at every turn. They constantly try to have the "last word" or the final comment on every issue.*
>
> *After a while, it becomes tedious to the men and they tend to shut down with the female. I have even observed women who use jargon that often sounds like two guys going at it in a school yard face-off. It looks a little ridiculous in the work setting.*

Toby is a top real estate broker, working in a female dominated workplace. He reflected on a woman's need to make her point:

> *Men tend to think negatively about a woman who may have a lot of knowledge about a particular situation and tends to be assertive in terms of really making the point...not only making the point but getting the point accepted, really pushing the point and driving it home. The male may feel left in the dust. He may think, I should know more...I've heard that...I get it...I'm not convinced, please just drop it.*

Outsmarting the SeXX Factor

Understand that you are worthy of the position and don't have to win at every juncture. Don't confuse confidence with obstinacy, stubbornness or inflexibility.

Let Him Run With the Ball...Who's in Charge Here?

The authors have attended thousands of meetings, conferences and symposiums throughout their careers. Some were interesting and others were drop-dead boring. A common style for small groups includes bringing in a facilitator. Good ones create an inclusive environment, adding to a team-building experience. Bad ones only facilitate chaos.

Renee is a vice president of Marketing. She described a situation that was excruciating for everyone in attendance:

Mark was leading a brainstorming session during a meeting at work. As people called out ideas, he wrote them down on a pad of paper. The group was lively and the ideas were coming fast. A female in the group became impatient; soon she got out of her seat, hung paper on a flipchart and began writing everyone's ideas there.

At first, Mark appeared grateful. But within minutes, she positioned herself in front of him and started calling on people for clarification. Eventually, he was literally edged out physically by her body.

In an obvious attempt to save face, he began outlining the ideas on the flipchart, positioning himself in front of her. It was clear to everyone that he was embarrassed that she was taking over his presentation. Others in the group (mostly women) tried to ask him pointed questions in an effort to bring him back to the forefront. It didn't work. The situation made everyone cringe.

Outsmarting the SeXX Factor

Even if you sense a male colleague may want your help when he's the one in charge, don't kid yourself. Not only will you look like you're doing a number on him, but you may be perceived as an appalling opportunist. It's not your job to rescue everyone in distress. You can ask if they would like an assist, otherwise, hold back.

The Year of the Woman...Big Girls Don't Whine

There are women in the work force who obsess over the parity of males to females in certain jobs. They make comments such as:

We only have two women vice presidents.

When will they ever promote a woman auditor?

Let's see...there are ten males and three females.

Men and women both know the statistics. What women don't always know, however, is how angry men can become every time a woman mentions this issue. Men do not want to be reminded about the lack of women in top management positions.

Outsmarting the SeXX Factor

Continue to lobby for female colleagues in a positive manner but do not make a public issue out of every position that you feel should have been filled by a woman. Choose your battles carefully. Getting women in key areas is always smart—it should open the pathway for others to follow. Not every position is a gateway though; choose—and support—the ones that you think will create more opportunities for women.

Is There a Doctor in the House?...Who's the Boss?

Women have climbed the ranks of professional organizations and achieved promotions through hard work and participation in advanced degree programs. They represent 50 percent of the students in the professional schools of medicine, dentistry and law. With every increase in knowledge, their self-confidence is strengthened. Yet women may not be aware that in their attempts to prove their worth, some often overdo it. A group of male executives attending a conference expressed how a woman's need to prove herself often alienates those around her:

> *Catherine is one of our female vice presidents. I knew that she was finally getting "it" when she changed her office around so that anyone who came in didn't have to sit across the desk from her. I think that often the female executive, administrator or manager tries to assert her authority in subtle ways. The message she was sending is,* I'm the boss and you're not.
>
> *I think Catherine is very ambitious and she feels the need to let people know she has worked hard for her position and has successfully beaten out the other males in the organization to reach this success.*

George, a CEO in a media company commented on the extensive use of titles by women in the workplace:

> *What is it with all these nameplates, college banners, and diplomas on the wall? We know who you are: "Dr. so and so"...you don't need to advertise. Look at my desk—I have no nameplate. If they don't know I'm the boss, they should work elsewhere. I don't need a nameplate or fancy stationary with "Dr." plastered all over it to prove I'm successful.*

Outsmarting the SeXX Factor

Moderate your compulsion for college diplomas, framed certificates and plaques on the wall. Hide the banners and use your title with discrimination.

Asleep at the Wheel...She's All Work and No Play
Are there written rules that women must work longer hours than men to appear qualified and competent? No, but there are unwritten rules. Many women work grueling hours—it's not uncommon to see twelve- and fifteen-hour days. Why do they do this? Is it that they can't complete whatever work they take on? Why is it that by Friday the guys at work plan TGIF get-togethers while women load up their briefcases and head home for the weekend? Ironically, just a decade ago, this was the male scene—long hours, work at home, little time for play.

Carrie presently holds a key position in an advertising agency. She revealed that her workday may not be ideal. She commented:

> *I work a fifteen- to sixteen-hour day. There's too much work to be done. I admit I am tired and don't know how much longer I want to continue at this job. I do know, however, that if I slack off, I won't move up in this organization. That's just the way it is.*

Most women in their pursuit of power often stand to lose the very essence of what made them successful in the first place. Women are burning the candle at both ends. They cannot continue to work twice as hard as men in today's workplace. For one thing, this workaholic behavior can be life-threatening. Statistically, more women than men have heart disease. And, statistically, more women will die from heart disease—the number one killer, ahead of lung cancer, lung diseases and breast cancer—than men will.

Furthermore, most men are not working like this. Thus when women work long hours, men report that it makes it appear as if they are not doing their jobs. Men loathe the comparisons which are being made in many organizations. Their bosses wonder why "she" burns the midnight oil while "he" turns out the office lights and goes home.

Sam, a manager of a mid-size business, commented on one woman's endurance record within his company:

> *My boss is beginning to wonder what's up. I've got a family and I like to get home regularly to spend time with them. My work is done and it's done well. That new female associate down the hall is always the first one here in the morning and the last one to leave at night.*

Women must be very careful. Many are working at a point of no return. They work too hard. They are making men look bad and causing men to resent them.

Outsmarting the SeXX Factor

Try not to confuse overworking with competence. Workaholics may win promotions at first, but will not be able to endure the pace. Besides, women who work too much look desperate. Often men think women who work *too many* hours are compensating, because they can't do it in the normal nine.

Ask yourself the question: *Do I really need to do all these projects or am I overcompensating for my lack of confidence?* Jot down the amount of hours you work each day in your planner. Try to reduce the time you spend at work a little each day until you are working the same amount as your successful male colleagues. Pace yourself and take time to smell the roses and have a life.

Men Believe in Street Smarts...She's a "Know it All"

Many men interviewed noticed women's needs to prove themselves or affirm that they can hold down a position successfully. This suggests that some women may need to prove that they have "succeeded" or "made it" into the upper ranks of jobs once reserved for males. One male explained that many women use their exceptional knowledge base to prove themselves in the male arena:

> *Women are competing for positions and there is a perceived need to overkill, overdo, overstate and overcompensate for real or perceived class positioning. There continues to be this behavior among women who tend to overkill with their knowledge base. It is a real turn-off.*

Another man provided a similar example:

> *In a recent interview for an upper level job, a woman applicant went on too long about every single aspect of her knowledge about the job. Her knowledge base seemed to turn off the males on the screening committees who then reacted in their own predictable way...she got bypassed—it happens over and over.*

Outsmarting the SeXX Factor

Slow down. Use your extensive knowledge in small doses. Moderate your urge to practice overkill with "how much you know."

The Queen is Dead...The Male Harem
Picture this: a talented, intelligent woman works hard to get to the top. She's good, but doubts herself and her successes. She still doesn't think she's that good. She lands job after job and almost manages to climb to the top. Along the journey, however, she begins to create a hive of drones around her—all men. Acting as her subordinates, they rarely leave her side. The woman believes "her guys" make her look more powerful and relies on them to help her succeed. What she doesn't know is that everyone in her organization talks and makes jokes about her "contingency of males." Everyone knows, but no one ever dares to tip her off.

One female CEO referred to this as "The Queen Elizabeth Syndrome":

> *During her reign, Queen Elizabeth gathered about her a contingent of males to do her bidding and used her power in a most unfavorable manner. I've seen this same scenario more than once throughout my career.*
>
> *There is a tendency for some females who have gotten into positions of power to have what I call the equivalent of a harem of men around them. However, it is not very flattering for the female. The dissonance from the males is mixed with fear that their livelihoods or advancement is at stake if there is not compliance.*
>
> *There's this uneasiness that the men are involved in something that is not appropriate and doesn't feel right for them. But, if they don't comply and/or support her, it's off with their heads!*

Outsmarting the SeXX Factor
If you're prone to using men to help you, know that others may begin to regard this dynamic in less than a positive manner. Employ caution concerning the "collection" of men around you.

Make Room For Mother...Hey, I'm Your Equal
Two male executives discussed situations in which women tried to control the men who worked for them. One said:

> *There are some female supervisors who patronize the males who work for them. It seems to be a grade school "teacher to student"*

relationship instead of a "supervisor to employee" one. The male turns off...he doesn't want to be dominated by the female. He thinks, Hey wait a minute here. I know you are my supervisor, but I perceive myself as an equal rather than as a guy in training.

The other executive added:

I can think of situations in which the woman acts like the man's mother. She thinks—I know what is best and this is how it should be, *as opposed to coming across as his peer.*

Outsmarting the SeXX Factor
Look inward and ask yourself some serious questions. Do you want to control this man or do you want to work in a collegial relationship? Exhibit exceptional caution when confronted with the urge to "mother" any male coworker or subordinate.

Confidence is the key to how you learn, how you grow, how you respond to adversity, how you present yourself in the workplace. It's not genetic, nor is it served to you on a silver platter. Confidence is earned. It comes through the school of hard knocks, from making mistakes, failing and living life. Who you perceive as the most confident men and women in your environment may not be so; you may not be regarding the true picture.

Everyone has bad days, weeks, months, sometimes years. It's an individual's confidence factor that will enable her or him to evaluate and grow and, at times, "bluff" friends and colleagues until normalcy is once again achieved. You, too, need to stretch and grow. Mistakes and faux pas will happen along the way. Some will be contributory SeXX Factors and create roadblocks; others will be minor potholes. In the end, they all become part of your personal collage—it's your experiences and how you handle them that will redirect you onto the confidence path.

Her Take:

I asked a male member of my committee fighting breast cancer what his ideas were about an important issue that would affect many people. He offered a thoughtful response and I gratefully used his input to make an extremely difficult decision. Later, I didn't understand why he got annoyed and hardly spoke to me.

His Take:

Why did she bother to ask me for my opinion if she wasn't going to use it? She knew what she was going to do. She was trying to patronize me. Why bother asking me. It's a joke.

9

War Games:
The Battle of the Sexes on New Fronts

Men's confusion with women's new roles is present on all levels. On the one hand men hear that women should be free to make any career or life choice they wish. On the other hand, they hear that traditional values need to be reinstated and that women should stay home to care for children because families are suffering from a lack of maternal support. Boundaries at home and work were once clearly drawn for men. As the boundaries disappear, men, who once defined themselves by their occupations and the masculine role of earning a significant portion of the family income, now find their confusion mounting.

As more women enter new arenas in personal and business environments previously dominated by men, their roles will demand new expectations. Understanding why men experience the SeXX Factor helps women to understand how men have defined their *own* gender roles. Society allows little variation when defining what it means to be a man and few cultural differences exist when considering the word "man." When people think of males in most societies, they think of him as the protector, provider and procreator.

Says Ronald F. Levant, Ph.D, in *Masculinity Reconstructed,*

> *Men have been drilled in the skills that men traditionally have had to draw upon in order to be able to work and provide for their families. It was about teaching us to be self-reliant, uncomplaining,*

aggressive, cool-headed, pragmatic, logical, resourceful, action-ori-
ented, goal-oriented, good at problem solving, good at strategizing
and good at giving every endeavor our all.

Men are still very much committed to fulfilling the traditional
male-norm requirement of being the good provider—in part because
so much of their sense of masculine purpose depends upon it, in part
because it's one of the few ways they traditionally have been allowed
to demonstrate their love, and in part because that's what they do
best.

It is no surprise then that the men who were interviewed said they feel confused about women who enter their formerly all male bastions as peers; they are even more confused when women turn out to have the top roles. Not only do most men find competing with women to be a new experience, they sometimes feel that they, not women, are the victims. As a result, some men still use the excuse that women are being promoted or gaining prominence in organizations and business spheres due to affirmative action or because they have been given special preferences.

Role Expectations...Let the Games Begin

Some of the men in the authors' surveys and interviews also reported feeling manipulated in sexual ways when they compete with women. As we've seen in chapter 5, some men believe that women use their "feminine ways" or feign helplessness in order to appeal to the male ego, whether it's their male egos or perhaps their bosses' or superiors'. In other words, they play by different rules.

A woman must keep in mind that many men's major source of self-esteem is closely tied to what they do, their jobs and the incomes they generate. Men naturally feel that women's advancement into their domain gives less credence to their power base. This invasion into their roles as providers and protectors causes men to feel out of control and decreases their self-esteem.

Here are five instances that cause men to experience the SeXX Factor.

Behind Closed Doors ... Are You Talking About Me?

Every year, all the male principals in Marilou's former school district take a trip to Las Vegas. They have done this for as long as anyone can remember. The stories are part of the school district's culture. No woman principal has ever attended nor have they ever been invited to go. No one makes a big deal about it, but many of the women principals feel left out. Four years ago, more women were being promoted to principals and the percentage of female to male principals grew to almost 50 percent. The women needed their own Las Vegas.

Marilou worked with a female colleague to plan an exciting weekend retreat at a spa in Ojai, California. Most of the women administrators attended and have continued to make it a yearly event. The group of women later nicknamed the group **WOW,** to stand for **W**omen **O**ff **W**ork. The men in the organization immediately found out about WOW and secretly renamed it **W**alk **O**n **W**ater, a term often used by the men to refer to many of the high achieving women principals. Some of the men thought the name was so amusing that whenever they observed a planning session for the weekend, they would walk by the group and yell "WOW" in a loud tone.

Soon it was reported that the men had named their all-male group trip to Las Vegas, "MOM." "It's upside down for WOW," one male reported. "We call ourselves "Men on the Move!" Their behavior was all in good fun, but the women soon realized that the men were feeling uneasy with the WOW group. A male colleague later confided that most of the men were unsettled about WOW:

> *Most of the guys wonder what you women are talking about on your weekend away. Are you talking about us or what? That's really why we kid you so much. Some of the men think you might be planning things we should know about.*

Another female executive commented on women's involvement in female dominated organizations:

> *Belonging to women's organizations that overtly exclude men... unless they start getting more and more men involved... creates a certain discomfort for men. I came to the conclusion that some women's organizations may not be a valuable help to women. The men are wondering, 'What are these women talking about?'*

Outsmarting the SeXX Factor

Understand that men feel threatened and left out by female dominated organizations. Don't flip the coin—we all know that women have been excluded from male clubs for decades. The smart thing to do is to invite them as well—many will decline, but some will enthusiastically join in. Our experience is that the men do bring good information and unwritten rules to the table.

It's My Manliness We're Talking About

One male CEO reported that he felt women held an unfair competitive advantage in the workplace. This male administrator actually believed...

> *I'm a good-looking guy, I come across well in public, everybody loves me...I've bought three new suits and now I think that I should be promoted.*

What men don't realize is that the female has done her homework and has prepared for advancement through education, workshops and networking.

Most men interviewed expressed anxiety and frustration when they discussed having to compete with women in the workforce. Few men, however, equate this emotion with anger, but rather indicate that they don't feel they should even have to compete with women. Researchers report that men, unlike women, define themselves through their work and, conversely, use work to define their manliness. But both men and women view work as necessary to supply the basic needs for survival and they believe, with luck, work will also prove to be a pleasurable pursuit. Willard Gaylin, a renowned psychiatrist and researcher, summarizes in his book *The Male Ego* how men and women differ:

> *For men, unlike women, work fulfills a third essential purpose; it defines his manhood. Even when work has been stripped of all joy and even when alternative sources of income are available (a working wife), the idle man sees himself as incomplete.*

Outsmarting the SeXX Factor

Be aware that men often define their manhood by the title they hold. Also know that women are perceived as encroaching on their sense of manliness every time we gain another high level position. Sensitivity and open dialogue about these issues with men at work can defuse a ticking potential eruption. If men sense that we understand what they are feeling, it lessens their subconscious anger and resentment toward the presence of high-level women in the workplace.

Double Jeopardy…He Thinks He's Smarter

Do you ever try to show men that you know more than they do? This behavior rates fairly high on the SeXX Factor Meter. Marvin is on the executive team of a publicly held telecommunication company. He observed:

> *There was this situation at work where one of my female employees volunteered to report on a subject she felt needed additional clarification. Jody was right on target or so everyone thought.*
>
> *Bart was the senior executive we were responsible to. He began to fidget in his seat, pursing his lips in an obvious sign of frustration and anger. We later figured out that something like this was going through his mind…Didn't she know that he was the expert? What was she thinking, trying to challenge his expertise in public?*
>
> *He listened to her detailed analysis of the situation for a few more minutes and then gave it to her with both barrels: "Perhaps when you've been around long enough and can see the big picture, you'll begin to recognize that all of your facts are just facts and have no bearing on the real issues." Her boss had leveled the playing field by exhibiting his own put-down of her in public.*

It's pure and simple. When a woman displays a level of knowledge that a man does not have, and he's supposed to be the expert, the man will never acknowledge the fact that she may have a superior level of expertise.

Outsmarting the SeXX Factor

You have the "know-how" and the "knowledge." Be cool. Don't use it against a male in public.

Down and Dirty…Using the "B" Word

A female CEO talked about her responsibility to supervise those in her employ:

One incident immediately comes to mind in which a male employee's use of profanity caused some of his colleagues to become offended. As an administrator, my responsibility was to have an intelligent conversation with this fellow to discuss his inappropriate behavior at work.

I scheduled a conference with him and sincerely thought things were going well in the conference when all of a sudden he looked me in the eye and announced, "Can I go now? I feel like I'm talking to my mother." The man later changed his attitude toward using inappropriate language at work. However, it is important to note that his initial response when confronted by a woman in power was one of frustration and anger. I later heard from my friend that he was calling me, "The Bitch from Hell."

As more women gain positions of authority, more men are being forced to deal with female supervisors. It's fairly simple logic: most men do not associate power with the female sex role. Entry into the social order for females has meant that they are expected from the very beginning to defer to males, to accept the leadership of males and to subordinate themselves to males.

Men's attitudes toward women in power often causes them to experience frustration, anger and confusion head-on. One of the most difficult tasks a woman in power must undertake is challenging a man on his inappropriate behavior at work. Confronting the situation is important and the technique you use is key. If you're not careful, the wrong method in confronting and dealing with it can bring out the worst in a man.

Outsmarting the SeXX Factor
When confronting a male subordinate on his inappropriate behavior or actions at work, take it slow and easy. Avoid chastisement or blame at all costs.

Giving the Order
A female vice president of a bank recently disclosed the details of her conference with a male security guard regarding his poor job performance. During her evaluation session, the security guard could not

keep eye contact with her nor could he agree with any of the woman's recommendations and strategies for improvement. She later found out from other employees that the security guard was making some definitely sexist comments about her at the bank. She became extremely angry as she confided to Marilou that the security guard had also unleashed the ultimate weapon that a man has over a professional woman, by telling everyone that she was a "man-hater."

After talking with Marilou about why she believed the man had become so angry with her after the conference, she disclosed that perhaps she had been too rough on the guy. She confessed that she had been reluctant to call the security guard on each and every problem as it occurred. Rather, she had saved up all her complaints concerning his poor job performance and presented them to him in one conference. She agreed that it must have sounded to him as if he were the world's worst security guard.

Power, according to most men, has been associated within the male context. Since many men associate giving orders with attempts to establish a "one-up position, in other words, to dominate," the situation becomes especially sensitive when it is a woman giving orders, says Deborah Tannen, in *Talking from 9 to 5.*

Men often fear the female invasion of their power, which causes them to have further negative thoughts about powerful women. This is especially true when a woman issues a direct order to a male. To give a man a direct order, such as "I want this done by Friday" or "Never leave your post unattended," can translate into real resentment toward not just the women asking for the task to be done, but women in general.

Outsmarting the SeXX Factor

When supervising a man, remember to confront any indication of his poor performance immediately. Try not to allow little things to build up to the point where you can't take it any longer, blowing your cool with him.

Women in positions of authority often make their male employees feel threatened, says Deborah J. Swiss in *The Male Mind at Work: A Woman's Guide to Working with Men.* One college professor did a comparison:

I've almost always worked under a woman. And when I finally started working under a guy, I felt myself saying, "Wow, what a relief." It felt so much more relaxed. I felt less was at stake.

What was the difference?

I felt more judged by women. I felt they were working out issues with power whereas the guys felt more comfortable with it.

War games were simpler when you were a little girl—but they existed. From the start, most women knew, as you probably did, that there was something awful and awesome about boys. They always hung around in a group, they played sports all the time, they spit and at school they were always chosen first to carry the American flag in an assembly. Nothing has changed, except your awareness. Boys aren't awesome—something to be awed—after all. Your perception has changed and with it your power.

The next chapter delivers the steps to learn how to keep from blowing all that power at work and in personal arenas.

He's aggressive...

She's pushy...

10

Shifting Gears: It's a New Attitude

Men have been forced to shift gears in their private lives and work lives, as they encounter women who have moved into top power positions. For many men, this sense of shifting gears is a major cause of the SeXX Factor. Since most women have been absent from high-level management positions, women typically have not been characterized in terms of power, status and leadership ability.

In the workplace, many men experience confusion with the sex-role spillover in their interactions with professional women. They are confused by the new and evolving female role in the workplace. Sex-role expectations are often reinforced by everyday interactions that keep women in "support and service" roles while men continue to assume "command and control" roles. Men's expectation that a woman's role should be one of support and service often triggers the SeXX Factor.

In the home, if men find that women can no longer be depended upon to provide total child care, cook all the meals and do the laundry, some get annoyed. This is especially apparent as men interact with women who choose not to fulfill these traditional sex-role expectations.

Hugh is a senior manager with a computer company. He is a perfect example:

I've had to interact with a lot of powerful women in my day. One thing that would definitely help these women is for them to stop being so emotional. And what's wrong with making a pot of coffee for the group?

Marilou uncovered numerous different situations that caused men to shift gears with the new evolving female power structure at work. As men experience these feelings associated with the SeXX Factor, they wish dealing with it could be so much easier.

Catch 22…She's Got Balls

Here's how it goes:

- Men hate it when a woman makes a tough decision like a man. *It's unnatural,* they say.

- Men hate it when a woman doesn't make a tough decision like a man. *What's she doing here if she can't cut it?*

This issue is hard to resolve. Working women *and* stay-at-home mothers must make decisions every day and are evaluated on their ability to make good ones.

Susan, a vice president of a large corporation, shared the following reflections about making tough decisions:

> *It's a lose-lose situation, so to speak. When I make the big decision that takes a lot of courage, I hear the gossip throughout the halls. "Wow, she's got balls," they say. When I make a decision that everyone likes, they say, "She's too weak…A man would never have done that." Men just don't understand how ridiculous this all is. I'm in a catch-22. I can never win.*

Do you think there is a difference between being aggressive and being pushy? To be aggressive in the world of work is to be assertive, domineering, determined, dynamic, energetic, enterprising and forward thinking. We are told that male workers are aggressive, but female workers who show the same traits are "pushy." These women have crossed the line into male territory.

Bridgette echoed what many women report:

> *I know a man and a woman who display similar leadership styles. At work, he is referred to as a "stern taskmaster" while she is labeled "hard to work for."*

This type of attitude toward the assertive woman in the workplace often causes men to experience the SeXX Factor. The big question is,

How can I show the organization how good I am and that I know what I'm doing without being too assertive? When women push or "show their stuff," men perceive them as too aggressive. Men, on the other hand, are expected to show high levels of aggression in their everyday work environment.

Outsmarting the SeXX Factor
Men can't control their feelings when it concerns any type of female aggression at work. Become aware that most men will probably have difficulty with assertive women. Show your male colleagues that your behavior is deliberate and purposeful. Also, your knowledge that men are put off by your ability to make tough decisions will help men learn to come to terms with this issue. Make your decisions and stand by them. In addition, sometimes share your thoughts with others on how it was that you came to your decision.

Your Highness...She's the Boss
Men are still getting used to the idea of women being in power positions. They read about it in the newspaper, they know it's out there, but many are still uncomfortable when the time comes that they have to report to a female superior. The concept of a woman having control can be disconcerting to them. They set up all kinds of tactics to deal with their role confusion.

Rhonda, an auditor for a New York accounting firm, remarked on one such tactic that she felt undermined her authority and added to men's confusion:

> *One of my male employees greets me every morning with, "Hi, Boss, how are you doing today?" We have a positive work relationship and get along on most issues. However, this man cannot call me by my first name or, for that matter, by my professional name. It's always Boss. Several female colleagues I have spoken to say they have also noticed that many of their male subordinates call them Boss.*

Patricia, an owner of a successful travel agency disclosed that she felt one man called her *Boss* in an attempt to downplay her power role.

> *I was always struck by the fact that this particular man often called me "Boss." It was an easy way for him to be the male and still be*

supervised by a female, I guess. I never heard him call his male supervi-
sors "Boss." I wish now that I had corrected this man up front, the first
time he did it, and requested that he call me by my actual name.

The confusion that men feel toward women who play the roles previously assumed by males is extensive. Men appear to experience the
most confusion over stereotypes they hold toward females who try to
assume roles that were once predominately slotted for males. Allowing
men, in support positions, to develop tactics that undermine your
authority only adds to their ongoing distraction toward you as an equal.

Outsmarting the SeXX Factor

If a male colleague refers to you as "boss," stop him dead in his tracks.
Initiate a conversation that may go something like this:
    She: My friend, why do you always call me *Boss?*
    He: That's simple, because you're the *Boss.*
    She: I know that...but without sounding offensive, I've got to tell you
    that I hate to be called *Boss.* Could you just call me by my first name?

New Girl in Town...Hey, We Were Here First

Can you recall an occasion when you were with some friends and suddenly a newcomer was introduced to the group acting as if he or she
had known everyone forever? How did you feel when the new person
began to monopolize the conversation or take center-stage? You felt
uncomfortable and embarrassed for her, didn't you? This same phenomenon can happen in work and personal spheres when a woman
enters an "all boys' club." Recently, this occurred when women golfers
tried to enter the all male club at which the Augusta National is played.
    Michael is an automotive executive. He told Marilou about an occa-
sion when he was working for an organization predominately staffed by
males:

It was the best time in my career. The men worked together to
make things happen and to garner awards for the corporation. Then
they hired a "hot shot" from outside and she changed everything. She
came in and abused her position (she was too full of herself). It was
resented...she made a lot of changes because she believed things
weren't what they could be. "Who is this young lady," we asked,

"coming to our workplace with all this power and support from upper management?" We out-right resented her.

Ed isn't keen about some women in the charity organization he has long supported. He openly commented about his animosity toward a particular female he called the "new woman on the block":

Anger cannot describe how most of us felt when the organization hired a female head. She came in with an agenda that blew us away. What's wrong with asking the old-timers a few questions about how things work around here?

Outsmarting the SeXX Factor

Your awareness of the organizational culture is the key! When you are the "new woman" on the block, spend time getting to know the ins and outs of the organization. This is just good sense. If you're walking into an "all boys club," raise an eyebrow or two and test the waters before overhauling what "worked for them." Build trust among your new colleagues before making any swift changes.

Rhinestone Cowgirl…Serious Vs. Froufrou

In the movie *Working Girl*, the secretary Tess (played by Melanie Griffith) is covered from head to arms with jewelry—all kinds of it: big, bright and noisy. When she meets her new boss Katherine (played by Sigourney Weaver), she immediately realizes that she has overdone it. To the ladies room she goes to delete the excess bangles.

Appearances do impact and influences others—it doesn't matter if it's at your child's soccer game, in the workplace or at the grocery store. Both genders react. Rhonda, a stay-at-home mother related the following story about a candidate for president of the Parent/Teachers Association at her child's school:

The female candidate ended her talk smiling. She appeared confident that she had done well and had a shot at the job. When I asked the current head his opinion of the candidate, he said, "She's very qualified, but she was wearing those dangling earrings and clunky bracelets that jangled every time she made a point." He also commented that he didn't take any woman seriously who wore jewelry like that.

Wayne is a supervisor in a company that manufactures paper products. He elaborated on his similar take on a woman at his company:

> *A female administrator I know has rings on every finger and three earrings on each ear. People thought she was cute and sweet and admired the work she did. But I don't think the males in the organization took her very seriously, because she dressed in a froufrou kind of way…not only can this be seen as a lack of power but it can be distracting to the men.*

A male executive related another story:

> *Sarah had everything: looks, talent, intelligence and, more importantly, the drive to get ahead. She was incredible. Most of the men in our organization tried to imitate her work behaviors. She recently interviewed for a top post in our company. She didn't get the job. The reason—her fingernails were too long! Some of the men on the screening committee made jokes about her "scratching their backs." I felt sorry for her. What talent lost for this organization… over fingernails… When will this inequitable treatment end for women?*

Outsmarting The SeXX Factor

Froufrou attire and accessories at work or in organizations cause many men too much confusion. They can't equate ultra-feminine style with serious endeavors. Avoid extremes and wear clothing and accessories that don't draw attention. Your attire in professional and other serious domains should call attention to you, not to your clothes and jewelry.

Macho (Wo)Man…Gender Bender

Some females, especially in the workplace, imitate the traditional style of the traditional role model; they begin to dress and act more like men. Many females in positions of power emulate typical male behaviors as a logical career survival tactic. In addition, some women work so hard at this game that they manage to be manlier than the men. Vivian, a life insurance agent, reflected on her fears:

> *A few years ago, I believed that women who acted and looked more manly than feminine were promoted to positions of power by*

males as a plot to deter the rest of the women in the world from ever
wanting those jobs. I really thought I had hit on something important!

I would observe a female colleague change right before my eyes.
Her wavy, fashionable hair would revert to a slick bun held back
tightly with a gold clasp. Her once "on the edge" fashion sense soon
drifted towards the masculine as she adopted dark suits topped off
with wire-rimmed glasses. I wondered if she was secretly getting hor-
mone therapy to keep pace with the men in the organization.

These women prevented me from ever wanting any top posi-
tions...I didn't want to trade my feminine style just for career
advancement.

Brian, an executive at a software company, commented about the
inconsistency of the female directors at his place of work:

The women in this place really kill me! One day they're wearing
tight, sexy dresses and the next day, black power suits. I just about
died the other day...there's this one gal in here who wore shoes that
looked exactly like the ones I was wearing. What's going on?

Women who depart from the norms of their own gender are viewed
negatively by males and peers alike. To succeed, many women have
fought long and hard to become more like their male role models.
They have become aggressive and competitive, wearing dark suits, consciously lowering their natural soft speaking voices and often outdoing
the men in the "stories they can tell." The concept that "we are equal"
has come to mean, "we are the same." This misconception often causes
some men (and women) to believe that women are losing their
integrity. Men continue to be confused by the new evolving female role
in the workplace.

Women wonder how this should all work. They want to maintain
their femininity, but are not taken seriously when they wear a long, frilly
skirt to work. Some women think the black suit says it all: power, or "I
know what I'm doing."

It's not all bad news. Mike owns a personnel agency. He spoke about
a female executive he knew who should give us all hope:

I know a female CEO and she has no trouble being a woman,
acting like one, expecting a man to respond to her as if she were a
woman. She knows what most men are comfortable with...a woman

who knows who she is. When I walk up to her, we usually embrace and welcome each other, that kind of thing. She is very sure of her own femininity and she acts like a woman. She is very successful.

Outsmarting the SeXX Factor

Seek out a critical friend and latch on to him or her as fast as you can. Ask your friend a hard question…Do I look or act like a man?…Do I have masculine traits, clothing or style? If your friend confesses that indeed your appearance has a masculine edge, take a good look at yourself in the mirror.

In addition, solicit the help of a professional fashion coordinator. She'll help you lose the dark, manly suits or suggest a more tailored, impressive look for you. Pay attention to what successful women wear and observe how they carry themselves or speak. Start to imitate some of these behaviors.

Finally, look inward to find your natural level on the continuum of gender identity (masculinity/femininity) and stay there. Moderation is the key!

Never Let 'Em See You Cry

In one of her interviews, Marilou asked a retired Army sergeant why women were once not permitted to join the military. "It's because of their tears," he answered. "Not only does crying hinder their ability to perform, but the other men are distracted by a woman's obvious distress and want to help. Besides, a soldier can't go into battle with tears in his eyes. He might not see the enemy."

Whether they are soccer moms or female executives, women who cry in their interactions with men of authority cause men to experience all kinds of negative feelings. The common prevailing male attitude as a result is that men get *angry*, while women get *emotional.* In addition, many men at work report that they're uncomfortable when they give women any constructive criticism. When asked why they were uncomfortable, the men all agreed: the major reason they do not confront women is their fear of women's tears. While there is not a lot of crying at work, it is well known that women are reported to cry in front of supervisors more than men do. If there was one single thing that men consistently responded to when asked what negative triggers they had about interactions with women, crying was number one!

Joe has worked in investment banking for twenty years. He spoke about women who cry at work:

There are some really talented women executives in this corporation. I've seen some of them come to tears. I'll have to admit, while on the one hand I think that crying is just part of being feminine, I think there's no place for tears at the top. I lose all respect for these (crying) women who think they can then go for a top position. It just doesn't happen.

Perhaps the "fear of tears" rather than the actual crying paralyzes men and keeps them from giving honest feedback to women both at work and in private interchanges on issues. Men want women to stop being so emotional, because it causes them confusion with the sex-role spillover. Crying, or the fear of a woman crying, strengthens a man's perception that women are vulnerable and not worthy of power.

Outsmarting the SeXX Factor

If you cry at work or during interactions with men on personal and family issues, a lot of men will have sympathy for you and try to help. However, you'll lose out many times on gaining your goals. If you think you're going to cry, use this technique...it works every time:

Roll your eyes up into your head and look up toward the ceiling.

You will immediately lose the urge to shed tears. It really works. Try it next time you get the urge to cry. Remember...cry at the movies, cry at home, but never, ever cry at work!

Playing the Field...A Friend in Need

Men reported that they feel unnerved by women who express the need to create close personal working relationships with peers and subordinates at work. Men who work with women know that women value friendship. They also recognize that women look for validation from these friendships and interpret this as an extreme lack of power and competency in the workplace.

Erica, now a corporate executive in the airline industry, talked about her need for friends at work:

I once befriended a male subordinate. I was enchanted by his level of intellect and his ability to help me generate positive change at work. We dined out at restaurants with our spouses and spent pleasurable days on his boat.

I needed him as much as he needed me. I relied on this man to validate that I was normal...that a position of power really didn't personally separate me from my staff.

Don't believe it. If you are the "Boss," nothing you do will ever make it any different. His income and, more importantly, his choices regarding his career depend upon your perceptions about him. I now believe that it's best to find friends at places of leisure or in your neighborhood.

Richard, a CEO of an accounting firm, remarked on his belief about women's friendships at work:

Women who need to have everyone in the office like them are at a real disadvantage. Their need to be liked by everyone really sticks out to the men. I think it distracts them from making the good decision when they need to. They don't want to end up hurting anyone's feelings. In my opinion, it's women's greatest undoing in the workplace.

Outsmarting the SeXX Factor

Make friends with colleagues who hold similar power positions to yours. It's lonely at the top and do not think you're a failure if you suspect that your subordinates don't like you.

Heart of Gold...Killing Him with Kindness

Do you *think* when in pursuit of serious goals for yourself and members of your family or do you *feel*? Many of the men interviewed cited examples of females who constantly talked too much about their feelings at work and in organizational settings. These feelings, the men maintain, get in the way of good decision making and clear thinking. Women care too much at work about those who are sick, those who may be depressed or those who may have family problems. This kind and caring attitude often translates into a lack of power at work. While most men claimed to appreciate having someone at work care about them, they still said they didn't want to hear women they work with talking about such matters.

Sid works with one of the major air shipping companies. He clarified his perceptions toward women who "feel" too much at work:

I think that males are uncomfortable with women who speak with too much emotion in their voices...or who talk too much about their feelings as opposed to facts. Women in power positions can't seem to shake these kind, caring, emotional female traits.

On the one hand, it makes them more approachable; but on the other, it can go too far...especially when decisions have to be made.

Outsmarting the SeXX Factor

While everyone knows that it is better to work for or with someone who cares about people rather than treating them poorly, caring in the workplace and other organizational activities can be taken one step too far. Men see too much kindness and caring as evidence of women trying to gain their positions by illegitimate means. Moderation of this emotion will go a long way toward eliminating SeXX Factor issues.

The "F" Word Isn't Female ...%!$%&#!*##!@#*

Women who curse and swear at work are not taken seriously by men. Men that we have interviewed over the years confess to being put off by any woman who swore.

Bob, a foreign rights literary agent, pretty much summed up what the great majority of the men said:

I'm old fashioned and I really hate to see women asserting themselves by being vulgar, attempting toughness. My daughters have learned that they can achieve their goals by remaining feminine and that they needn't be loud to be heard.

The majority of men that Marilou interviewed reported that they lose respect for a woman who curses or swears at work. Todd expressed his uneasiness when a woman let loose at work:

You know it's funny. When a female curses and swears, I think she's doing it for effect. If a man curses I receive it differently than from a female. At work, you expect to hear it from the males, but you don't hear females using vulgar language. It's really disturbing.

Don't be fooled for a second. Women who act like men using slang, swearing and telling dirty jokes are widely disliked by males and females alike. Men, however, do not hold their male colleagues up to such high standards. The 'Double Standard' for men and women is still very much alive and well at work and in private arenas.

Does trying to fit in and be one of the guys backfire? For Veronica, it did. John works for a large law firm. His take on what happened:

> *Veronica was the best. She would go to all the retreats with the men and after a few drinks, she would tell these hilarious dirty jokes. The men loved them and enjoyed having her around. But when it came time for top-level promotions, she was always associated with those dirty jokes. The top power guys just couldn't shake it. She never got past the in-house paper screenings.*

Outsmarting the SeXX Factor

Women who successfully interact with men in and outside the workplace as they move forward in their careers and personal arenas, usually have collected an arsenal of favorite words and jokes. Save them for when you're with close friends or when you're alone in the car. Try to break the cursing habit altogether if possible, because when you land at a certain frustration point, "Fuck," comes out too easily. If you can't break the habit, try substituting the word "shoot" for "shit," which most people find acceptable in the work place. Using words like "shit" or "fuck," (even just once) on the surface may make you appear to be one of the guys. They say, "Wow...she's only human...she's just like the rest of us."

The truth is, if you're on your way to the top you are *not* like the rest of them; *they* expect and want you to be different.

Call It Culture...He Wants Me to Curtsy?

So what's the big deal? Let a male open up the door for you if it's appropriate. What are you trying to prove? Some women make issues over common traditional male courtesies that have been socially accepted for hundreds of years.

Many men experience discomfort when it comes to mundane things as opening a door or stepping back in an elevator so that women can exit first. Alan, who works in aerospace, observed:

> *The classic situation that causes men uneasiness is when he wants to open a door or take charge of something that a man customarily does for a woman and in response, the woman says, "No let me do that, let me open my own door" or "I'll take care of those*

*arrangements." That's something that has evolved as more women
enter the world of male dominated professions.*

Gail is the president of a large national charitable organization. Her
position demands that she attend multiple meetings each day.
Recognizing that there are not many women in her position, she felts
the need to constantly show that she is in charge. She commented:

> *When I was first elected to a position of leadership that was tra-
> ditionally held by males, I needed to show that I could do things
> myself without help. At the time, opening my own door was symbolic
> of the position I held. Consequently, I would rarely allow any man to
> open up a door for me or help me carry heavy packages. I worked
> with a male associate who would race to open the door for me and
> hold it as I walked through. I would later try to beat him to the next
> door so that I could open it myself.*
>
> *One day, he finally couldn't stand it any longer. He ran to the
> door and said, "Hold it. This is killing me. I need to open this door
> for you. This is how I was brought up." We laughed and agreed to
> both relax. We decided that we would "practice" with one another to
> act natural when we approached the door together.*

Outsmarting the SeXX Factor
When you associate with old-fashioned men who want to use the traditional male/female courtesies, just do it. Let them get the car for you
when it's raining...let them open up the car door, let them order the
food for you...let them pay...let them tip...let them stand up when you
leave the table, let them do all of those things they have been taught by
their mothers to do for women.

Do, however, become mindful of where such men stand on these
issues. Watch their actions to sense their approaches to such issues. For
example, if you get the feeling that he expects you to split the check at
lunch, he'll give you a sign, such as leaving the bill on the table a little
longer than normal.

It's All In The Grip...He Likes it Medium-Rare
There's nothing worse than a man with a lifeless handshake. A million
things go through your mind; one can sense the uneasiness. A man feels
the same way when a woman shakes his hand with a powerful grip.

Professional women have a tendency to take on characteristics in leadership that males often perceive as unfeminine. Males assert that women who succumb to these male stereotypes will not make it in today's work world. Most men interviewed agreed; successful women are first and foremost very much women.

Russ discussed the uneasiness he experienced when shaking hands with women in positions of power:

> *Women should use a looser grip when shaking hands versus a firm one that you expect from men. Many men feel uneasy when a woman casts aside feminine norms and shakes your hand in a gruff, masculine way. It doesn't feel right and men don't particularly like it.*

Not all women have weak or wimpy handshakes; and not all men have strong and firm handshakes. Sometimes men, and women, hold back on "quality" handshakes with others who are deemed of lesser or little value. A handshake, though, relays information to the person it is extended to. It can say "I'm glad to see/meet you," it can say "You are nothing," or it can say "I don't really want to be here."

Judith was a presenter at a national conference in Atlanta, Georgia last year. One of the other speakers was the former UN Ambassador, Congressman, Mayor and Co-Chairman of the Centennial Olympic Games in 1996, Andrew Young. As he was introduced to the other speakers and board members, his handshake was not impressive, to say the least. Everyone went away with a non-enthusiastic feeling that flowed over in their take on his presentation.

Outsmarting the SeXX Factor

Give yourself the "handshake" test by asking a close male friend to grade your grip on a scale from "way too limp to bone-cruncher."

What's the bottom line for women who interact with men at work or in private spheres? Play it smart—make moderation the norm, from the handshake to the jewelry to the independent attitude. In the long run, what do you really gain by creating friction and animosity in the office or your private life? Work to create a positive atmosphere in which you can move ahead and attain your goals.

What the dinosaurs went through after that meteor hit the Earth,
that's what men are going through now.

– Dr. Ronald F. Levant,
Masculinity Reconstructed

11

Culture Clash:
Challenging the Dominant Male Norm

Needless to say, men have been the dominant gender in many power cultures for a very long time. In recent years, though, women leaders are working their way up and into that power culture, bringing their own ways of doing things with them. Some also have begun to demand and receive special considerations. In the workplace there are things such as maternity and child-care leaves and in other domains such as sports, clubs and associations, full inclusion into previously exclusively male activities. Even though men say they ascribe to equality and fairness, they are often confused by the new paradigms: career women who want it all—fast-track career success and children—and women who want men to be equal partners in child rearing. Many men still believe that women should have to make a choice: either work or stay home and raise a child.

The reluctance of men to acknowledge women's multi-dimensional roles as wives, mothers and executives has contributed to men's irritation and discomfort when they interact with women in social activities or at work. Six instances may trigger the SeXX Factor in these areas. Confront and challenge some of the heretofore unchallenged rules and norms of arenas which in the past have been male dominated.

Who Invited You?
Harry, an executive with an insurance company, reflected upon a story which disturbed him:

*I had the occasion to observe a female executive as she directed
the janitor to hang a unisex sign on a former male restroom. She
appeared to find satisfaction in the snickers of the men watching
and seemed to enjoy their discomfort.*

Women are finally getting accepted into the "old boys club," a
male bastion that has created and shared the nuances and unwritten
rules within and outside of the workplace. It's not impossible for
women to be included, but it isn't easy. Many men feel more comfortable with other men and are malevolent toward women who they still
may perceive as intruders trying to enter their domains.

Men experience anger and frustration especially when women try
to gain access to places of power brokering, such as golf courses, card
rooms, bars and even the male restrooms. While most women know
that many opportunities for advancing their goals arise over lunch, on
the golf course or in the locker room, women who want to move
ahead in their careers and personal activities must be aware that many
of these areas are still "sacred cows." It's a fine line when deciding how
far is too far to push. Women often risk alienating men to reach those
places of power formerly reserved for men. It then becomes a no-win
proposition.

Outsmarting the SeXX Factor

Appreciate how sensitive men can be over the issue—it was "our" place,
scene, etc. and now it's "theirs." Moderation and feminine sensitivity are
crucial when trying to gain access into former male bastions of power.

He Wants to Play with the Kids Too

William summed it all up…"I am sick and tired of women who want it
all." He expressed his frustration and jealousy over some of the new
advantages for women in the workplace and personal spheres:

*I am married and have two kids. My wife and I both have to
work, because it now takes two incomes to raise a family, purchase a
home and have the amenities necessary to live a good life. But I have
to say, I don't like this double standard. Women want time off for
caring for sick children, child birth, etc. I would like to spend time
with my kids during the workday, too. If women want men to be*

equal partners in raising children, men have to be given equal privileges; but if I ask for time off to assume the role of caretaker for my children, I'll be derailed or viewed negatively by my superiors.

Outsmarting the SeXX Factor

Women must continue to request and work for special advantages in the workplace such as leaves, flexible scheduling and child-care provisions. But they must do so for *men and women alike.* Trying to have it all at work or in one's personal life makes many men angry and resentful about women who say they want the power.

I Want It My Way

More irritating to men than women invading traditional male-dominated places is that now women have created their own avenues to broker power. They meet at concerts, gyms, spas and women's clubs, and at meetings of service organizations, churches and synagogues. Many men are now beginning to know what it feels like to be left out. As a result, women are feeling the backlash.

Bobbi is one of the top real estate agents in her office. She summed up this dilemma:

> *Women are going to have to develop places to broker power that include men and that are non-threatening to them. One thing that will keep a woman from progressing in any organization is duplicating the behavior that men have exhibited in the past...such as the need to exclude those that are not like them.*

A Family Affair

Most men like to keep work and home life separate. Most women, on the other hand, have difficulty separating the two. Jennifer discussed the ways in which women inject female rituals into the male culture at work:

> *A good example is how the female worker loves to observe birthdays, holidays and anniversaries at work. On secretary's day, I gave my secretary a very expensive, significant gift. The word spread like wildfire throughout the organization and three male executives came into my office and exclaimed, "You paid enough for her to hire a housekeeper for a day! Thanks a lot. Now what are we supposed to do?"*

The males come from the "have to" and (we) come from the "want to." I realized later I put the men in my workplace in the position that "I'm up here and they're down there." In doing so, I made them look and feel bad, which hardly leads to fruitful interaction on other issues.

Mark is a computer analyst. He was amazed when a new hire literally transformed her assigned space which was open to all since the front wall was glass. He adds:

We recently hired a new director of marketing for our company. I was stunned yesterday when I was called to her office. It looked like my family room at home. I mean it…she had frilly curtains hanging up, she's wallpapered some sunflowers in one area, and then, in the corner were a few stuffed animals. Come on—where's she going with this?

Outsmarting the SeXX Factor

Realize that men feel uncomfortable with the new female shift within and outside the workplace. Think twice before you decorate your office with lace curtains or give lavish gifts when you know you are "besting out" the men in your organization.

Nothing Personal…He Needs His Space

One issue the gender books don't talk about is that of a man's physical and personal space. Most men especially like to keep it to themselves. They do not want anyone to intrude without permission. This, of course, includes women. Their space can be an athletic event, a meeting, in their office or even just having a casual conversation. Most women, on the other hand, will allow others to enter their space without hesitation.

If you observe men and women in conversation—be it woman to woman, man to man, or woman to man, the physical positioning of the interaction gives much insight into their communication with one another. When a woman talks with another woman, it's not uncommon to observe constant eye contact, reaching out and touching each other on the arm, leaning toward each other—as if to share an intimacy—and a more open body language and facial expressions. When women are done, they then break away.

When a man talks with another man, his eye contact is not constant, it moves around; rarely will you see either man reach out to touch the other; they won't lean in as if to share a confidence; and their bodies are closed off, with arms crossed or hands in pockets. When they are done, they don't need to break away; they are already separated.

Ken reports that he likes women, but he experiences discomfort when women enter his personal space at work:

> *If there is one thing that drives me up a wall, it's when a woman intrudes into a group and moves up real close, putting her face within six inches of mine when she wants to say something. I remember one woman who even tried to follow me around a conference table with a roller chair. It was ridiculous. I would slide back and she would slide toward me with her chair. I thought it almost comical but she was insistent on getting into my space, for whatever reason.*

Joe echoed Ken's comments and added his own about women's "open door policy":

> *When I think about an open door policy at work I think about being more open to my employees about ideas...not literally that my door is open. The women I've encountered seem to think that they can enter my office space without permission. I have a hard time addressing this with our female employees. They barge in and start talking... "Do you have a few minutes?" I want them to ask for my consent before entering my office.*

Outsmarting the SeXX Factor

Give men the physical space they need to feel comfortable interacting with women. Pay attention to where their sanctioned territory begins and ends. Whether it's in their offices, on golf courses or in their neighborhoods, you won't win points by invading their personal turf.

A New Twist on the Old Double Standard

Do women have it all? Do they have a choice to work or not to work? Depending upon whom you talk to, many feel that women work to get out of the house. In truth, most women in today's society have to work. They may be single mothers, the sole breadwinners; they may be part of couples, where the second income is necessary to pay for necessities for themselves or their children; or their spouse/partner may have been laid off or disabled.

Despite these truths, many men still feel society favors women. "Women have it all," Mack grumbled:

> *They can have their fast-track careers, their kids and the whole thing. Take me, on the other hand…I have no choice. I've got to work for the rest of my life. I don't have the same options open to me as women do. No matter how much things may change in society, it's the guy who's ultimately responsible for his wife and children. I couldn't take time off for a second to raise my kids.*

The anger that men often have comes from knowing that women do have a lot of choices that they don't have. For example, most women know that they can take time out to have children if they are fortunate enough to have a husband who can support them for a while. Men, on the other hand, know that in most cases this is not possible for them. While they truly want to provide and care for their families, their frustration at knowing that few escape hatches exist for them rankles.

Outsmarting the SeXX Factor

Understanding that men may harbor feelings of anger and frustration and knowing that they have few choices relative to their long-term employment status is important when interacting successfully with them.

Confronting the gender differences that cause friction between men and women inside and outside of the workplace shouldn't be viewed as a necessary evil. Men are unique, so are women. They are different in their interactions with their own genders as they are when interacting with the opposite sex. The examples cited in this chapter should be considered "general"—you most likely know exceptions in each scenario, as do we. But when looking at the big picture, it appears many of the complaints voiced by men have some merit as do the complaints raised by women. However, since women seek to "raise the roof" in formerly male arenas, we must be aware of the potential complications and how we can mitigate them.

You women just don't get it. When we men set somebody up, we take care of them when they get out.

– Bill, Security Guard for the
Oprah Winfrey Show

12

Women in the Male Bastion

Many women today are continually placed, and work, in the so-called Velvet Ghetto—workplaces that have a majority of females versus males employed. The dynamics of a female-dominated workplace vary from a more integrated or male-dominated workplace.

Velvet Ghetto workers include secretaries, administrative assistants, cashiers, bookkeepers, accounting and auditing clerks, nurses, nurses aids, dental hygienists, dental assistants, social workers, flight attendants, K-12 school teachers, waitresses, sales and retail workers, child-care workers, librarians, receptionists, hairdressers and manicurists, public relations specialists, residential real estate agents, publishing personnel, textile sewing machine operators, general office clerks, bank tellers, housekeepers and maids and computer operators.

In previous chapters, it was noted that some of the SeXX Factor triggers for men are women's chattiness, the collectiveness of women and their hinting/assuming that men (and others) know what they want or are thinking. In the interviews, comments also surfaced often about mothering, nervous giggling, playing dumb and even overusing fragrances.

When one gender is dominant, whatever it is that bugs the other, will be, or at least appear to be, exaggerated. Isolated incidences don't act as triggers. But, when a trait appears to be more female than male and it is displayed within a female-dominated workplace, the trait can be magnified. Shannon and Mary, female physicians, revealed:

Our male colleagues comment on the "chatter" of the nurses and how they constantly talk over each other. Where the women view it as casual conversation, the men also get irritated when women rattle on rather than get to the point.

Men hate it when women give out personal details about themselves as well as people they don't know or have never met. It's common for women to share details as a type of enrichment of their experiences. Men's take is: "So what?"

Bob, an international trainer and author, routinely works on team building within organizations at the middle management level—a level where there will likely be more women, versus at the senior level. He recalls a time when he was working with several women on a project:

One turned out to be a bit on the lazy side and her lack of performance during a particular job turned out to hurt us. Afterwards, another woman said to me, "See, I told you she was lazy." I said, "No, you didn't. You never told me that." To which she responded, "Well, I was giving you hints." Well, I never got the hint. I suggested to her that the next time we are working on a project and she needs to tell me something important, she should just TELL ME instead of hinting.

Patrick is a critical care nurse, working in one of many female dominated workplaces. Even though he enjoys the humor and playfulness of the women in his department, he noted that there were times that the giggling was out of control.

Women who laugh in response to almost anything pushes my buttons. This is usually a high-pitched, nervous giggle that has no connection to a humorous stimuli. They seem to laugh at or about everything.

Brad is a computer expert. He doesn't have a problem with anyone—man or woman—who doesn't understand all the components of technology. What does bug him is when someone plays the "dumb routine" or "Woe is me." Brad explained:

One trigger is when women act dumb or like little girls in the hope of getting the "big, strong man" to do something for them. Just a couple of weeks ago a woman said to me, "I'm just a dumb blonde," when she wanted a technical favor from me.

Clark is a successful coach, working with the football team that took regional championships many times during his career. His wife, Louise, teaches in the high school as well. He's the first to admit that there are things that bother men. At the top of his list was strong, fragrant perfume. He will actually avoid events if he knows that there will be lots of women, all decked out. His words:

> *I don't know what it is with women. They've never heard the saying, "A little goes a long way." I've attended many events with Louise where several of our fellow teachers are also present. There are far more women in teaching than men. Collectively, all the perfume they have on is enough to gag you. It's a real turn-off.*

Where Clark and Louise have been in the teaching professions for several decades, Torri has taught for only five years. In her brief experience, she has formulated opinions that echo Clark's and Louise's:

> *From my experience, women in teaching want it all. They want to be nurturing Martha Stewarts under the umbrella of being a hardcore professional. So they "mother hen" any man who also works at school. Most of them can't pull this combination off well and end up looking like flakes and that irritates men. For example, when this "type" makes a decision that will affect a faculty member (male), she will always ask his opinion in her sweetest little "teaching" voice. Men don't respond well to this.*

Leslie is the founder of a successful Midwest training company. Her clients are mostly corporations. The comments she observes in the behavior area that are triggers for men also revolve around mothering. It's not uncommon to see women displaying a maternal reaction to men, and only men. She clarifies:

> *It amazes me that so many women treat and react to men as if they were their mothers. They treat them as if they are children—you shouldn't do this or shouldn't do that; be sure to take your coat; here's an umbrella, it's raining; don't eat that...it's not good for you.*

The Unwritten Rule Rules
Once, Judith was the guest "expert" on *Oprah* to discuss her book *Woman to Woman—From Sabotage to Support*. As one of the panel members was telling her story about being undermined and betrayed by another

woman, Judith waited behind the curtains prior to her introduction to the viewers and audience. She soon struck up a conversation with a security guard and was amazed at the unwritten rule the man shared.

As they both viewed the monitor, he said, "You women just don't get it." When she asked him what 'get it' meant, his response was, "When men set somebody up, we take care of them when they get out."

She never forgot his words. In 1992, when Ross Perot was on *Donahue* during the presidential campaign, Donahue asked what Perot had told Oliver North during the Iran-Contra hearings. Perot responded, "I told Ollie to tell the truth. If he went to jail, I would take care of his family, and when he got out, I would guarantee him a job."

Now how did that security guard from Chicago know what Ross Perot from Dallas knew? The security guard knew, as do most men, that if there is a scapegoat or a fall person, one of the rules—unwritten—is that you "take care of him when he gets out." And it seems that many women don't know this rule.

Outsmarting The SeXX Factor

Some women are reluctant to share information—information that could eliminate problems in a relationship, make one's work easier, or be the difference between survival and extinction. Pass on unwritten rules—those tidbits that you wished you had heard early on that no one shared.

More Than One's a Crowd

Women are far more likely to work and socialize closely together. It's called crowding. Men quip that in restaurants and social gatherings, women always go to the bathroom together. Because so many of women's positions are in the general workplace or in Velvet Ghetto environments, women's positions are often given a lower status. Lower status individuals typically get less space. With few exceptions, those who have power are more likely to have their own offices.

Secretaries and clerical workers often get no more than a partition, if they are lucky, or are placed in a "bull-pen" environment. When psychologists have studied crime, they have noticed that crowded living conditions in small spaces have a negative mental effect and are considered influential factors in the criminal's life.

This isn't just for criminals. Ongoing research shows that those who work in a very high-density condition, which includes high-level interactions, are more likely to feel hostile and aggressive. This is usually the case for women. Women are more likely to be accessible, even leaving their doors open if they have them, which leads to a higher interaction level with others at work.

Much of the sabotaging and bullying behavior that women report is generated from another woman is primarily due to their social conditioning in the cultural context of the workplace. Situations are created when some women feel hostile, aggressive and angry and take out their aggressions in covert and subtle ways. This compounds the feelings of low power and low self-esteem in other women.

When a woman is in a low status, low self-esteem position, she is more likely to be a target—a scapegoat—vulnerable to the workplace bully. One of the survey respondents wrote that her office had meetings where someone would be "it." The "it" person would be positioned early in the week by the manager. Cutting remarks and innuendos would be bantered about by co-workers until the regular meeting day arrived. This allowed the group to direct anger, remarks and negativism at the person of the week, deflecting such things from others. The "it" girl was got!

Women will most likely become the scapegoat candidates when anger surfaces. They are typically the low status members who have less power to protect themselves. They *are* "it." It's the easiest choice. Women don't sabotage and undermine other women because of genes or gender-linked characteristics. They learn it.

With the significant changes from the corporate reorganizations of current times, a classic situation arises: the survival of the fittest. Battles are fought by both overt and subtle manipulations. Many of the players, women and men, will be rendered obsolete. Obsolete in the workplace, obsolete in value, even obsolete in friendships. Some will come away dismayed and distressed and others will look at it as an opportunity to grow and expand in whatever they are doing.

Outsmarting The SeXX Factor

Don't get caught up in the group dynamics that female-dominated workplaces or activities such as school parent/teacher associations or "mother's" groups can create, including actions of betrayal, bullying and sabotage that are more likely to be activated by covert methods. Men are continually amazed that some women appear to be friends with each other, yet undermine their so-called friends.

Caution in the Salon

Lucille was grateful for the support of her staff when she was in the hospital. The fresh flowers, phone calls and visits assured her that her clientele was being taken care of after she had collapsed in her salon one day.

After a week of tests in the hospital, the doctors could not explain or identify what malady had befallen her. To her close friends, she confided it must be overwork. Her friends weren't so sure.

For several years, Lucille's salon had been one of the "best" in her city, as rated by the general populace. She had been supportive of all kinds of groups and causes in her community for the past fifteen years by donating haircuts, facials and manicures for the asking. Whatever group needed to raise money, she was there to support their cause.

When in the hospital, she appreciated her employees who visited her daily. One of them, Maria, went out of her way to be helpful—bringing paperwork from the office, tracking inventory, even giving Lucille a rundown of the type of services rendered to the salon's daily customers. She also would drop tidbits of the latest gossip that circulated within the shop.

When Lucille was finally discharged, the doctors strongly advised her to stay away from work for a month. Tough words for someone who is also the owner and the one who is usually the first in and the last to go home at night.

During her convalescence, Maria told Lucille that Sandra, another employee, had tried to add all the new customers and changes of address to the customer files on the computer, but was having trouble opening them. Appreciating the extra help, Lucille gave her the password. That one word shut down Lucille's business.

When Lucille got wind of what was going on from a former employee, she went to the shop and learned that it basically had been raided. Maria, Sandra and another stylist had walked out, carrying the detailed records of a fifteen-year-old business. They had opened their own shop armed with the particulars of Lucille's business and the names, addresses and phone numbers of all clients from the past five years.

Lucille's computer was still there, but with names and addresses deleted. Her inventory had been depleted and thousands of dollars worth of merchandise had been ordered in her name. The pile of bills was unbelievable. To ice the cake, a virus had been entered into the computer, infecting all of the files.

At its peak, Lucille's thriving business grossed in excess of one million dollars a year. After Maria's handiwork, the business went into decline. Eventually, Lucille declared bankruptcy. When she discovered Maria's duplicity, she felt betrayed, used and angry. Rightfully so.

With her health weakened, Lucille felt she had no energy in her to confront, much less combat, her foe. Rebuilding a business takes time, drive and positive support. She just didn't have it. Painfully, she closed her business and took her remaining loyal customers to another shop in town. Some of her employees went with her; for others, she contacted friends in the trade, assuring everyone of a "new home."

Lucille had been sabotaged by Maria, an employee she had hired five years before. What compounds Lucille's experience and the sabotages reported by many others is that Lucille and Maria work in a female-dominated workplace. Does this mean that sabotage is worse in a female workplace and/or is this a woman's issue?

Outsmarting the SeXX Factor

Be discerning with your trust and don't confuse friendliness with friendship. Before you open up, determine what type of values, desires, concerns and feelings you have in common. This won't happen overnight; it will take a period of time. If there is a commonality, then, and only then, should you consider sharing anything that might be construed as personal—be it access to your files, your computer or your secrets. Otherwise information about you will end up in cyberspace.

One of the major pitfalls women continually fall into is getting too personal too soon. Men don't. Women are more inclined to talk too much, be too open and tell too much about themselves, their fears and weaknesses too soon in any relationship with another woman. You need to learn that just because a woman is friendly, it doesn't mean that your life saga needs to be shared up front. Wait. Forget what your mother told you; you don't have to be friends with everyone. Friendships in the workplace should be construed as bonuses, not requirements.

Being Friendship Savvy

In *The Friendship-Savvy Quiz*, ten questions have been identified that you should ask yourself. These questions relate to working with women, women with whom you may develop friendships. If you answer *yes* to any of them, it indicates that when you develop relationships with others, your personal expectations carry a "strings attached" element. Women need to recognize that healthy relationships are necessities and friendships are luxuries. It is also imperative for women to understand that not everyone is friend material.

The Friendship-Savvy Quiz

1. Would you feel uncomfortable if you needed to criticize your friend/colleague's work?

2. Would you allow her extra time to complete tasks or projects?

3. Would you feel hurt or be angry if she took another position without telling you about it first?

4. Would you feel left out if she transferred to another department or moved to another city?

5. Would you feel excluded if she went to lunch with another and didn't invite you?

6. Would you feel overlooked if she forgot your birthday?

7. Would you feel bad or uncomfortable if she criticized your work?

8. Would you feel betrayed if she told a personal story about you or revealed anything that you considered intimate to others?

9. Would you feel uncomfortable competing for a position or promotion with her?

10. Would you cover for her if you knew she was having personal problems?

Source: *Woman to Woman 2000* by Judith Briles © 1999. All Rights Reserved.

These questions were designed both from the position of someone who manages women and for those who simply work with other women as a colleague or co-worker or on a project within your community or children's school. A *yes* answer doesn't mean that you shouldn't develop friendships, it just means there are some hooks—those attached strings. One yes or many yeses mean that you may have to be sensitive to your relationship; there can be hurt feelings that may spill over—domino-ing could (and most likely will) impact your as well as her and others' work.

Female-dominated workplaces are a challenge. They can be an excellent place to work when there is mutual respect and trust. Initially, women display warmth and openness to other women in their workplace. They often share confidences and assume that because they have, those confidences will be treated as such. The sense of betrayal felt is deep when any confidence is violated.

There's no doubt about it. Women are different when it comes to leading an organization, whether it's the parent/teacher association, a charity or an office team. One thing that annoys me is their inability to make timely decisions when it comes to important issues.

When a guy has to write a directive, he goes into his office, closes the door and writes it. Today, if a woman has the top spot, she usually runs around and asks everyone what they think about such-and-such before making a decision.

I've seen cases where a woman makes a decision and a few of her committee members or employees protest about what was decided ...the next thing you know, the decision is changed to suit the three or four upset people. This doesn't make sense to me.

– Howard,
Telecommunications Supervisor

13

She Works Hard for the Money: Mixing Mars and Venus

Men and women often define leadership differently. Research indicates men and women bring different leadership styles and skills in the workplace. For example, the command-and-control style of leadership is often preferred by males, while the interactive style is often preferred by women. Men find it difficult to recognize women as leaders when women use these collaborative, interactive approaches to leadership. Men criticize women for being too much team players, not being directive enough and for taking too much time to make decisions.

Women's new style of leadership—participative—has frequently been cited to be more effective in today's organizational environment. As a result, men have begun to experience the SeXX Factor in the workplace and in other interactions with women in their communities as they sense the style of leadership they have relied on in the past may not be the only one that will work in the future.

Here are eleven different female leadership and management themes that drive men to experience frustration, confusion and sometimes anger.

Beat the Clock...Is It Quitting Time?
From fast-food managers to presidents of major corporations, differences in leadership styles between men and women have been well documented. Contrary to popular myths, female administrators are just as effective as their male counterparts. For the most part, it can be

safely said that women have developed values and characteristics that result in behaviors that are different from the traditional, aggressive, competitive, controlling leadership behaviors of men. Women in managerial or leadership positions tend to bring developmental, collaborative and relationship-oriented behaviors to leadership.

Men think that collaboration in the workplace is too time consuming. Collaboration, for most men, translates into more time at work, more time in meetings and more work for them personally. Research, however, has shown that the collaborative approach to solving problems and including people in decisions is better for business.

The different female style of leadership prompts many males to experience frustration, withdrawal, anxiety, annoyance and discomfort. Pete expressed his frustration over a function being planned at his church:

> *Martha, the mother of one of my children's friends, and I are on the same committee at our church. We are working with a large group to decide how some money should be spent on our pageant. Martha has been very careful and stays in a problem-solving mode, listening to everyone's idea and charting all the options. She constantly asks everyone to "brainstorm." Sometimes I feel like my head is going to explode.*
>
> *This woman has everyone giving their opinion and working in small groups. I want to jump out the window. This is not rocket science; we've been doing this for twelve years. My feeling is let's get on with a decision. I've got other things to do.*

Outsmarting The SeXX Factor

Know that collaboration rather than competition is new for many men. Our research indicates that men eventually start to prefer this leadership style over time, so be patient and hang in there. One way to ease men's frustration is to explain your rationale for using collaboration with a particular issue. If you can logically justify your use of collaborative techniques, most men will generally appreciate it. Know that collaboration will eventually make him a "believer" in the team spirit.

Power Failure...He's Not Sharing

Jane reported that she had recently informed her supervisor that consensus building was one of her biggest accomplishments for the year.

Her supervisor nodded while she went on with the specific details. He then informed her that she was being criticized by many of her male subordinates. They believed that she was acting too much as a team player and not being directive enough with the staff on major decisions. He advised her to consider the following:

> *Just tell them what to do and they'll do it. Don't share your power with others. You are being labeled as "weak" by many of the males in this organization.*

When men indicate they want women to be more assertive at work, they may mean they want women to stop sharing the power with subordinates. Men and women exhibit many differences in leadership style. Male leaders tend to lead from the front, attempting to have all the answers for their subordinates. Women lean toward facilitative leadership, enabling others to make their contributions through delegation, encouragement and nudging from behind. Women prefer to work things out through team building.

Outsmarting The SeXX Factor

When you build teams, whether at work or in charitable or child-based organizations, you ultimately share some of your power. Know that this effective leadership trait causes men to believe that you have no power. Have open dialogues with committee, staff and other associates about what it takes to make a team. Model your sense of shared power to everyone while still maintaining a directive style on issues that need a strong focus.

He Likes an Instruction Manual...A Man with a Plan

Susan's path to the upper echelons of management was blocked by men who were uncomfortable with her more open, non-confrontational style of management. She was essentially told by upper management to change her style if she wanted to become promoted. Men in the organization had informed her that they tended to view her collaborative style as a weakness rather than as a managerial strength.

Mary, a stay-at-home mom and former school counselor, agreed. She reported how men had trouble with her style:

A short while ago, I asked my son's male high school teacher how he was going to solve the student discipline problems in my son's classroom. I tried to be insightful and ask probing questions such as, "Why do you think my son and other students are out of control in your room?" and "Why do your students talk when you talk?"

I wanted him to take some responsibility for what was happening and perhaps generate some of his own improvement strategies. He just sat there and looked at me with a blank stare. He actually said, "I don't know why these kids are out of control. Why don't you tell me; you seem to think you're the expert."

I tried to probe him again with more questions. He crossed his arms as if in disgust. I took this as a sign to move on and offered him a few of my ideas on how we could work to improve discipline both at home and in the classroom. He seemed almost appreciative. The light went on in his eyes; he was now a man with a plan.

Outsmarting The SeXX Factor

Share your style openly with male subordinates and associates in your work and personal life. Let them know up front that you want them to be part of the improvement process and share with them decisions and changes.

A Public Opinion Poll...Don't Bother Me

Women in management positions have learned that's it best if they obtain as much information as possible before making important decisions. Barbara, an administrator in an advertising agency, told about the problem men have with her style of decision making:

I asked a male employee what his ideas were about an important issue that would affect many people. He offered a thoughtful response and I gratefully used his valuable input to make an extremely difficult decision. He later confronted me; "Why did you bother to ask me for my help if you weren't going to use it?"

The problem with this strategy is that some men believe they are actually being asked for advice rather than asked for their opinion. Other men feel manipulated when a woman asks them for their input with respect to a decision. George confided that he felt betrayed that his boss (a woman) had made a decision after asking him for his opinion:

> *She was trying to make me think that it was my decision, but she knew that she was going to do what she wanted in the first place. Why bother asking me? It's a joke.*

Men continue to be confused both in the workplace and outside when a woman asks them for their opinion before she makes a decision. Women are known to take more time before they make decisions than men, because they take the human dimension more into consideration. Many women want to know how a particular choice will affect not only themselves but also those around them. Women want to ask questions and get as many details as possible before making important decisions. Men tend to want "a plan."

Outsmarting The SeXX Factor

Whether in personal or professional situations, some men think that women who ask others for their opinions before making a decision lack confidence. In your private and work domains, talk openly about the decision-making process with those who are involved. Let them know ahead of time that you may not always use their information but that you value their opinion.

What is She Saying?...Just Say What You Mean

People have different ways of communicating. Indirect communication—an issue mentioned earlier but worth revisiting here—can create problems between men and women. Examples include:

> *Is it too hot in here?*
> *Do you think the music is too loud?*
> *Is anyone hungry?*
> *Do you want that last doughnut?*

This indirect style is usually associated with females. Why do women do this? Many researchers believe that historically, women have had to use language circumspectly to get what they want. Today, in using a collaborative approach, some women still feel too afraid to assert their own desires, wishes or opinions. Communicating in a shy, coquettish manner enables them to get what they want without being perceived as too "pushy." Some women even believe that only an insensitive, uncouth person would need a direct verbal message to understand the speaker's meaning or point.

Men, on the other hand, are confused and frustrated with indirect messages. They prefer strong, purposeful, unequivocal statements, instructions or demands. The person who uses such direct language is viewed by most men as powerful, decisive and worthy of respect. Most men interviewed, on the other hand, perceived indirect statements as mere suggestions of a manipulative, weak individual.

Outsmarting The SeXX Factor

Avoid indirect, weak suggestions and try using direct, decisive statements. Here are some examples. Practice saying them and come up with others on your own:

1. *I think it's hot in here. Does anyone mind if I open this window?*
2. *I'm really hungry. Let's go to that Chinese restaurant down the street.*

A Crap Shoot…Did She Really Have to Ask?

Many men cannot subscribe to woman's collaborative leadership style that puts everything out in the open. Women tend to use a process that is more inclusive, one that allows more people to express their opinions or ideas. Men have operated authoritatively in the past and have made most of the decisions themselves. Women often expand the workload for everyone and risk weakening their power base. They have a tendency to take risks by bringing things out in the open, a strategy that can backfire if they're not careful.

Rita, the chairperson of a charity organization, talked about an incident that involved her need to collaborate and take risks:

> *A large group, including some important benefactors and board members, had been assembled to help make an important financial decision. Through my direction and facilitation over a two-hour period, the group finally came to consensus on how to spend an $80,000 contribution. I was overcome with joy. We had worked through the many suggestions and decided on three top areas of need where we should spend the money, including a few needed repairs to our offices.*

What a deal, *I thought.* This has been collaboration in its purest form. I'll give it one more shot to make sure I've covered all my bases. *I knew that everyone had come to consensus on the issue and felt fairly safe.*

"Okay," I said, *"Does anyone have anything else to add before we dismiss as a group?"*

No one spoke up. But out of the corner of my eye I could see Mrs. Peterson, a whining type, tilting her head to one side and then the other. She had been a thorn in the group's side throughout the entire process. She moved forward in her chair, with squinted eyes. I thought for an instant that she had gained her composure when she suddenly raised her hand and asked to be recognized.

"Yes, Mrs. Peterson," I whispered.

"Well," she stammered, *"I know we'd all like to go home but, uh... does anyone think that perhaps the Rotary Club might do some of the work for free? Because that would free up some more of the money to use elsewhere."*

We met for at least two more hours and decided to reconvene the following week. I think I overheard two men in the back of the room kidding about plotting my murder, along with Mrs. Peterson's.

Outsmarting The SeXX Factor

Remember they chose or hired you for "your" expertise. Try not to overdo your need to collaborate and include everyone. Most men want to go home at the first sign of any group consensus. One of their biggest power static triggers is when women keep going over the same thing again and again, things that were decided long ago.

Who Cares?...Touchy Feely

Years ago, someone created "icebreakers"—those activities that are done to ease a group into a process, whatever the process is. The intent is to loosen everyone up so that they are comfortable with each other. This is done through a group activity, a general get-together or some type of game that everyone participates in to create inclusion. Many companies and organizations send their women managers and committee chairs to training sessions to learn about icebreakers and how to use them. You will rarely see a man initiate an icebreaker at a meeting or in a public place.

"Icebreakers are demeaning," Tony, a male corporate executive, confided:

> *I think this is what women do at baby showers and wedding showers, but not at work. I do not want to divulge my deepest thoughts to a group of people that I hardly know. I don't even care if they know me. I do not want to sing like a pigeon, pretend that I'm a musical instrument or build my dream house out of toothpicks. I want to get this meeting over with and go home.*

Outsmarting The SeXX Factor

An excellent transition for teambuilding that men often use involves contests. Turn that icebreaker into an event or game with a prize (such as a lottery ticket) and you're home free.

Manipulation Is a Dirty Word...Persuasion Is Part of Her DNA

Many women know how to get people to do things for them or for their organizations. This is one of their greatest talents. A lot of men, however, get together in groups to discuss this very topic. "How did she ever get that guy to do such and such?" they ponder. "I could never have pulled that off."

Women know that often this is their key to success in interacting with men in their work and private lives. By nudging, persuading, including and cooperating, women often convince men that they are part of the process. Once they are involved stakeholders, most men will be active contributors. Most, however, will dig in their heels when they are not involved in decisions that personally affect them.

Richard, a teacher, works in an atypical school district; approximately 30 percent of the teaching faculty are men—much higher than in most elementary school districts. The principals are mostly women—there are eight women and four men. He discussed the way women's skills of shared leadership are often personally frustrating:

> *There are some guys who are very concerned about staying in control. Women, however, are more willing to share their power with others. As this becomes the preferred method, the male becomes frustrated, because he doesn't always perceive how the woman is working and guiding people.*

Men just don't understand how women maneuver people and
try to mold them and how gently they have to do that at times.

Outsmarting The SeXX Factor

Rule #1: While manipulation in its purest form is a dirty word in any-one's vernacular, many times it's part of our way of being a woman. Let's face it—we know that if we nudge, suggest or persuade a little bit, we can get men to cooperate. Just be sure it's not overdone or too obvious.

Be careful that men never begin to think that you are using them. Be true to your convictions and tell them the truth at all times. Show a genuine concern for the issues at hand.

Favorite Son...His Boss Likes Her Better

A man and a woman were both asked by their immediate supervisor to present to the Board of Directors their process for dealing with funds in their organization.

Trent's presentation was short, concise and very hierarchical and linear. His presentation took a little over ten minutes. Barbara's pres-entation was global, holistic and inclusive. She elaborated on how she had included all stakeholders in the process for deciding how the funds should be spent.

Barbara's presentation lasted a little over half an hour, three times as long as Trent's. Throughout, the supervisor nodded and smiled in agreement on most of her points. Trent became annoyed and upset listening to her presentation. He felt his presentation had paled by comparison.

Later, he spoke to his supervisor in an agitated manner, saying that he viewed Barbara's presentation as an intentional attempt to humiliate him. Raising his eyebrows, the supervisor commented on Trent's anger and embarrassment:

In discussing this situation with me, Trent was really panicking,
because he knew Barbara's way of collaborating with the employees
reflected my way of doing things. His real question to me was, "Does
my behavior fall short?"

This is not an uncommon situation. Men and women often display different leadership skills. Feminine styles of leadership building—that of collaboration, shared power and relationships—are becoming more popular with upper management as they translate into higher profits and more contented employees. However, many males feel threatened and annoyed with this new style that has gained momentum in the business world.

Outsmarting The SeXX Factor

If you sense the boss likes you better than another employee, because you and the boss think alike, be aware of how much frustration you can cause the men with whom you work. If you and your male peer are both on the line and you know that your behavior (or presentations, reports, etc.) will outshine him in front of his boss, give him a "heads up."

Bad Press...Too Good for Her Own Good

You've read it in the newspaper. You've seen it on television. You can even buy a best seller that will tell you that women have had to work twice as hard as men to succeed. Some of that is true. Some remains to be seen. The fact is that a lot of men are beginning to feel the pressure as they work alongside competent women.

When Marilou first became a school administrator, she was excited about the opportunity to make a difference at her school. At the time, she was one of only a few females commanding a large middle-school population and was quite proud that she had gained a promotion once slotted exclusively for males.

In the beginning, she thought she may have made the men in the school district look bad, not intentionally, but to prove something to herself. During the first three years of her job, she nearly killed herself creating new programs and raising the level of standards that would later be recognized at both state and national levels.

One of her male colleagues told her that the other male administrators liked the way things were at their schools and were beginning to feel pressured by their bosses to come up to her standards as an administrator. Most of the guys referred to Marilou as a "loose cannon" and did not want much to do with her on a personal level.

Mikell, a female colleague in Marilou's school district, felt the tension. She thought that women's more elaborate presentation skills made several men at work suspicious:

> *When a female makes a dynamite presentation, the men think to themselves,* This is not our thing. We have been here for a long time and it's not our bailiwick to do the dynamite presentations. What's her purpose, what's she up to? Is she trying to get pro- moted? What's the deal? *I sense that there is a real discomfort on the part of the men having to compete in this situation.*

Outsmarting The SeXX Factor

If you make him look bad, even unintentionally, you will eventually end up all by yourself. However, you need everyone with you in order to move ahead. So what's a woman to do? Keep doing...but take time to share your accomplishments with your male colleagues, associates, committee members and friends in similar positions.

For example, if you've just implemented a new process at work or in your organization that your superior is enthused over, subtly inform your male associates about it. If they seem interested, suggest that you would be willing to help them implement a similar process.

Details Drive Him Crazy...Don't Overkill!

Women are detail experts—most will say that they are multifaceted. They can effectively sort, categorize, synthesize, group, rank, coordi- nate, arrange, adjust, regulate, order, classify, systematize and even pigeonhole data. On top of that, they can walk, talk and chew gum at the same time! Men, on the other hand, prefer their data "straight up."

Carl summed up his frustration with female organizational skills:

> *I generally find women to be more detailed-oriented, better in terms of planning. This process takes longer, however, and can be a real pain and quite frustrating. Generally, I think most men get con- fused with all the data and organizational stuff that women put out there. A lot of what I see is not only unnecessary, it's overkill.*

Timothy views the female in action as a wonder to behold. He confessed that he often feels inadequate when compared to females who sort out the chaos:

We don't think like they do. I am fully aware that to be organized is to be more efficient but I am tired of looking bad next to my female colleagues who appear on the surface to have everything highly organized—from color coding to which Post-it® is appropriate for which file.

Outsmarting the SeXX Factor

You know how good you are with the details. Just don't jam them down his throat or draw ugly comparisons to his lack of organizational skills. No matter how hard men try, the majority can never come up to women's level of organizational expertise.

Study after study has shown that women have to work harder than men do to be viewed as competent as men are perceived to be. So women attempt to involve others in decision-making situations, work long hours, have co-chairpersons, are collaborative, like to lighten up—which could include an icebreaker or two—and are quite good at juggling multiple projects at one time. What's the big deal?

The big deal is that women need to practice a little of what Kenny Rogers sang about in *The Gambler*.

If you're gonna play the game, boy, ya gotta learn to play it right...

You got to know when to hold 'em, know when to fold 'em.
Know when to walk away and know when to run. You never count
your money when you're sittin' at the table. There'll be time enough
for countin', when the dealin's done.

An important part of the SeXX Factor is knowing the rules—whether for leadership, management or support staff, or when the playing field is your child's school or sports team, the workplace, a volunteer or charitable group or community activities. Gender dissonance traits make it difficult to work effectively with the opposite sex. Do any of yours? It's easy to say get over it... but it's far better to know when to hold, know when to fold and know when to declare, "This is not a big deal for me either...I can walk away."

Nobody likes me,
Everybody hates me,
Think I'll eat some worms.
Long, slim slimy ones,
Short, fat juicy ones,
Think I'll eat some worms...

– Childhood song

14

Resolving the Clash:
Stop Being Your Own Worst Enemy

Many of the respondents in our surveys indicated that at times they practice *self-sabotage*. This can include negativity, low self-esteem and confidence, not being able to handle criticism, having an aversion to risk, having a bad attitude, being narrow-minded, being careless, carrying personal problems to work, talking too much, blaming others for problems, being immature, not following through, passing the buck, being moody, avoiding negotiations, conflicts or confrontations, as well as being caught up in the "should of's," "ought to's" and "if only's."

Self-sabotage also generates the *terrible toos:* too nice, too agreeable, too naive, too quiet, too overworked, too afraid, too dependent and too guilty. These traits seem to affect women more than men. Before we go further, let's create a definition of self-sabotage.

Self-Sabotage:
The undermining of and resulting damage or destruction to personal and professional integrity and credibility *caused by one's self.* Any of this can also lead to the erosion and destruction of self-esteem and confidence.

Prior to becoming the producer of a popular morning television show in San Francisco, Shirley would have identified herself as a shy person. She wanted to go into television when she graduated from college—it was her dream job. Everyone she knew told her to start in a small town. Instead, she went straight to San Francisco.

First, she obtained an interview with Ryan, the program manager of a local radio show, who offered her a job as its producer. When she asked what the job entailed, she was told she would be responsible for contacting individuals and asking them to appear on the show. Shirley's words:

> *Ryan told me that if the mayor were involved in a breaking news story, I would call him up and ask him to be on the show the next day. I told him that I couldn't do that. I've never done it before and I didn't know how. I asked if I could start lower, not as a producer yet. My about-to-be employer quickly said, "Adios." It would be five years before I got another job in the business.*
>
> *During those years, I worked for several banks and I continued to go out for interviews. I finally landed a job as the receptionist at a local television station. Once in the door, I went to every department and offered my services. I'd say, "I'm just sitting here most of the time. Is there anything I can do to help you?" Gradually, I was given more work. I became a production assistant and made the same kind of phone calls I had panicked about years earlier. I also began to write movie vignettes for the local newspaper.*
>
> *As I got to know people in the business, I learned of an opening at the ABC television affiliate as the production secretary. It was only for a few months, as a replacement for a woman on maternity leave. I decided to go for it. I survived, stayed on, and eventually became the production secretary on the morning show. As the program grew in importance, so did I. A few years later, I became its producer.*

Outsmarting The SeXX Factor

The fear of failure, the fear of criticism, the fear of negotiation, the fear of confronting, even the fear of taking credit for accomplishments haunts too many women today. Self-sabotage involves doing things that are against your own best interests.

Common phrases such as *being your own worst enemy* or *shooting yourself in the foot* are often bandied about when self-sabotage is in action. Most of us practice some form of self-sabotage at some time in our lives. If you make it a habit, the result is self-defeat and sometimes self-destruction. Remember, opportunity doesn't always strike twice.

Battle Scars...She's Come a Long Way, Baby

Gail was fifty-eight years old. She managed to overcome several obstacles in her career to become one of the top vice presidents in her organization. She moved her home from state to state, working on her doctorate at night after a long day at the office. She traded having children for a career. Weary and tired from the fight, her wrinkled face and pursed lips said it all. Crashing through the "glass ceiling" was not an easy deed. The shattered glass caused visible battle scars. Gail was indeed an angry woman.

Many women have had to overcome several barriers to get where they want to go career wise and/or family wise. Some of these barriers may have involved overt discrimination against females. We all know that it has happened in the past and still exists in some areas.

In the professional arena, it's not uncommon to hear stories about females who continue to display aggressive behaviors in order to affirm their power positions. Marilou remembers one colleague who always seemed to have her boxing gloves on:

> One female felt that she always had to fight with some of the strong male administrators in the county. I think she looked for these fights. I told her that I respected her and asked, "Why do you have to constantly carry on that battle? Why don't you let some things go?"
>
> I later became aware of her history and how difficult it must have been for her to achieve respect in a previously male-dominated profession. She had to stake out her territory and fight with men to be recognized. But that's over now and she can't let it go.
>
> She's one of many seasoned women who have a chip on their shoulders from fighting battles to get ahead. Successful, younger women don't have this chip on their shoulders, because they haven't had to fight quite as many battles.

Outsmarting The SeXX Factor

If you harbor feelings of resentment toward males who have won positions over you, move on, and appreciate that many women are reaching goals never thought possible. It may not be worth it to wage the fight.

Check your urge to spar with a man who may have personally discriminated against you just because you're a female. Abstain from telling critical stories about why you think a particular man was chosen over you...there are millions of them.

Is There a Saboteur in You?

Self-sabotage exists in various degrees. On one end of the pendulum are individuals who are so destructive that nothing ever goes right for them and the people around them. Their careers and personal lives are a mess. These people are never happy about anything. You could call them nega-maniacs—they moan and groan about everything, wallow in self-pity and appear to enjoy it!

In the middle of the pendulum are those who act out self-sabotaging behavior on a periodic basis. It is not an everyday or weekly occurrence. But, once in a while, they really blow it and they know it.

At the other end of the pendulum swing are those who have displayed some form of self-sabotage, recognized it and made a concentrated effort to not repeat whatever was the behavior. Landmines in the workplace, on boards of trustees, in parent/teacher associations and other organizations are inevitable. Your destruction is not.

The following is a *Self-Sabotage Quiz.* Take a few minutes to read through it and answer every question. If you find some difficulty in answering or you're not sure, you might consider asking a trusted friend to give you appropriate feedback. Whomever you ask, there is a string attached. This person should be caring, supportive and non-judgmental.

Self-Sabotage Quiz

Directions:

Put the appropriate number next to each of the statements below that best describes your behavior. Score **0** for *never,* **1** for *rarely,* **2** for *sometimes,* **3** for *often,* and **4** for *most of time.*

_____ 1. If I'm given a challenging project, I expect to fail.

_____ 2. I spend time with people who shoot down my ideas.

_____ 3. I sometimes say yes when I really want to say no.

_____ 4. When I am complimented, I feel I don't deserve it.

_____ 5. I usually expect the worst to happen.

_____ 6. I often procrastinate until it's too late to meet a deadline.

_____ 7. If I am in a conflict with someone, I will give in to keep the peace.

_____ 8. Sometimes I think I'm whining, but I don't know how to stop.

_____ 9. When I make a mistake or something goes wrong, I tell myself how stupid I am or that I'm a jerk.

_____10. I am my own worst critic.

_____Total your scores by adding the values assigned to each response.

What your **Total** means to you:
The lower your score, the less likely it is that you are a self-saboteur. The higher your score, the more likely it is that you create and encourage conditions that bring about career setbacks, disappointments and failures.

0-8: You are in pretty good shape. You appear to have few tendencies that undermine yourself. It is also highly probable that you are a self-confident person and can handle most landmines in your work and personal life that come your way.

9-17: You are on the border and display some tendencies toward self-sabotage. You may sometimes speak before you have had the opportunity to gather the data and facts about a situation. You recognize the "mouth in motion before brain is in gear" scenario after it has occurred. One thing that you can do to help offset any self-sabotaging tendencies is to have a trusted friend signal you with a pre-agreed gesture or word when he or she perceives that you may be acting or speaking in a way that is leading you to hit the self-destruct button.

18-26: You are a self-saboteur. Many of your thoughts and actions get in your way. Scoring in this range means you are a master at negative self-talk, such as, "I always make mistakes; this is impossible for me to do; I knew I would blow it; someone else can do better than I can," etc. You are also a master of self-fulfilling prophecies. With negative self-talk, you can almost guarantee that whatever you perceive the outcome to be, will be.

27-40: Unless you are undergoing a substantial problem or you are under a great deal of stress, a high score in this area spells tremendous trouble. Your non-belief in yourself and your negativity is a major handicap in any advancement in your career or your personal life. You need positive support, not negative criticism. You need to put extra effort into removing yourself from others who are also saboteurs and nega-maniacs. The old saying that "Birds of a feather flock together" is quite true in this case.

Instead, focus your energy on positive affirmations and small victories—a succession of small victories can lead to major victories. Anytime you have a victory (arriving at a destination on time counts), acknowledge and applaud yourself. You have begun to take the steps toward eliminating self-destruction and self-sabotage.

Source: *Stop Stabbing Yourself in the Back* © 2003 by Judith Briles. All Rights Reserved.

Acknowledging that you are a self-saboteur is a major step on your road to recovery. Be willing to get outside help. You won't be the first person to enlist the help of a psychotherapist to help you remove the barriers you have erected throughout your life.

If you have ever gone through a difficult time, it is normal to have some self-doubt, paranoia, blame, low confidence, feelings of failure and feelings that you have been victimized, all emerging at some time. The phrases, "If only I had done this," or "Why is this happening to me?" are internalized and vocalized. Everyone has voices. Those inner, self-effacing voices can be so subtle that you barely hear them, yet at the same time, it's as if someone is shouting in your ear at close range.

Deactivating Self-Sabotage

When you are your own worst enemy, snares and traps are waiting to be activated—the active ingredient is you. All are situations and conditions that you manifest. Encountering these traps and feeling that your world may be caving in distorts your normal, everyday range of perceptions.

It does not mean you are going over the deep end, all is lost and you are a total failure. Landmines don't always explode. Recognizing that inner traps exist and that there are solutions to them means that you can deal with self-sabotage issues.

SeXX Factor Traps
Following are several traps we've identified that consistently surface for women. Decide which ones get in your way.

Low Self-Esteem and Self-Confidence: A lack of self-esteem and confidence prevents you from stretching, reaching and seeking new competencies and challenges. The recovery and growth of confidence is one of the foundations for living. Without it, you will be held back from acknowledging and correcting any of the SeXX Factor inhibitors. Chapter 8, *Confidence Crisis*, offers tips to kick-start your confidence.

Miscommunicating: At the base of most problems is the simple fact that communications go astray. Women and men have different takes on words, body language, events, even jokes. Add in differences that are created from varying generations, cultures and races, and the verbal soup gets quite complicated. By using words, jargon or phrases that "don't fit," you set yourself up for a misunderstanding that can trigger any of the SeXX Factors identified in earlier chapters.

If you communicate directly about what you like and do not like, as well as what constitutes unacceptable behavior around you, you'll find that you'll gradually feel that you are back in the driver's seat, taking control. Once you take control, and recognize that you're in charge of your own destiny, the SeXX Factors won't be of concern to you.

Negotiation Avoidance: Not understanding and utilizing negotiation techniques can lead to both personal and professional disaster. Women are upset about not getting paid the same as men; the simple truth is that too many women will accept less pay for the same amount of work and fail horribly at negotiating for what they want. For many women, negotiating is equivalent to conflict and therefore should be avoided. Learning how to negotiate will resolve conflict, not create it.

Viewing negotiation as a matter of cooperating and resolving a problem versus creating a conflict is one of the first steps in creating a negotiating mentality. Negotiation plays a key role in your workplace and personal life. The most important step in any negotiation process is to be prepared. In any negotiation, 80 percent is planning and only 20 percent is action.

Being prepared means knowing what you want and also knowing what the other side wants. You should be able to clarify, if you get what you want, what's in it for the side that concedes to you. You must have a clear picture of what your goal is in any bargaining process. Without it, the outcome could be significantly different from what you desire.

Fear of Failure: Failure is a judgment about events, either yours or someone else's. When failure occurs, the results are often the loss of self-esteem, money and social status. Anticipating or expecting too much, too soon, in any endeavor can lead to failure. Anticipating or believing that you will fail can almost guarantee it will happen.

Successful men and women are separated from those who are not successful by their attitudes about failure. People who are successful don't fear it. They don't like it either, but they recognize rebirthings can happen, and, for many, they may pronounce it one of the best things that's happened to them.

For whatever reason, failure happens and it happens to the best of people, rarely once, but many times. The key to growing out of failure is to learn from it.

Fear of Confronting: Being unwilling to confront, even acknowledge issues, sets you up for negative self-talk, failure, even paranoia. Key factors to keep in mind in confronting is first, to recognize that whatever conflict created the confrontation does not necessarily mean that you are in an abnormal environment. Conflicts arise daily from living and working with others. It is how you manage the conflict and the confrontation that will make the difference.

The person in any confrontation who is the better listener usually wins. Listening is a skill that is not learned overnight. An expert listener listens with her eyes and her ears and pays close attention to the words, tone, gestures and body language of the other party.

You will address a series of conflicts throughout your life. By avoiding them, not confronting them, self-sabotage multiplies. You move yourself into a victim mode, blame problems on others, reduce your confidence, avoid any type of negotiation, enhance negative self-talk and procrastinate about any type of commitment because of the fear of a future confrontation. It becomes an insidious chain of events. Reread chapter 6, *Yakkity-Yak*. In it are several tips on how to be a better communicator.

Being Too Personal: Divulging too much personal information to others can lead to gossip and the belief that you are a blabbermouth and not able to maintain confidences. It can also set you up for being sabotaged by others.

Two of the growing-up messages you most likely heard was "be nice" and "be friends." Those messages often lead women onto the path to being too personal or to over-personalizing situations. There is no question that women talk about a greater range of topics—we talk about our hopes, dreams, aspirations, relationships and blunders, to just about anyone.

If you work in one of the female-dominated workplaces described in chapter 12, *Women in the Male Bastion*, you know that a woman's tendency is to be too open and sharing—long before she has had the opportunity to evaluate or determine whether others are entitled to her trust and confidences. Until you know for sure what someone's style and pattern is, you should think about how and what you share with her or him. Ask yourself—how would this look on the front page of the newspaper or shared globally via e-mail? If you wouldn't like it repeated, don't share a confidence—keep quiet.

Being Vengeful: Plotting and planning a get-even approach dilutes your energy and derails your work and personal life. "Hell hath no fury like a woman scorned," and, "Don't get mad, get even," are common phrases heard for years. Planning, plotting and acting out vengeful action is usually a direct result of anger—yours. Being angry does not mean that you are unhealthy. Everyone at some time is going to feel anger. It is how the anger is directed and whether it's healthy or unhealthy.

Any acts that are rooted in anger are delivered in a variety of ways. Consider the most common piece of equipment in the office outside of the telephone—the computer. Incredible degrees of destruction can be generated from deleting files, inputting erroneous information, introducing viruses, sending libelous and slanderous messages throughout a network; you name it, it's been done.

Consider the rumor mill and gossip. Reputations, credibility, empires can be brought down with a few well-placed words. Believe it or not, gossip is probably the most common form of revenge.

Women also use gossip to connect with other women. In effect, it acts as a builder of self-esteem, though most likely the results are temporary. If you know some tidbit about someone else and believe that others would like to tap into your information, you get a momentary boost in self-esteem.

Gossip can be likened to a pool, but not the kind of pool in which you swim laps and feel refreshed when you get out. The gossip pool is like a cesspool, the more you are in it, the smellier and more unpleasant it becomes. Gossip that is destructive and vicious is created from misdirected anger. It's a way to let off steam.

Negative Self-Talk: Negative self-talk sets you up for failure and an erosion of self-esteem and confidence. Any type of negative self-talk, from "I'm a jerk for blowing the presentation" to "I'm worthless and shouldn't be alive" is destructive and paralyzing.

When your inner voice says that your idea, your concept, your work, your friendships (whatever it comes up with) are useless and have no value, you infect yourself with a virus. That virus sets up a progression of thoughts that literally says that your ideas are dumb and stupid and a waste of everybody's time.

When you fill your mind with statements like, "I am too young, I am too old, I don't have the talent, I didn't go to college, I can't use the computer, I can't type, I can't..., I can't..., I can't...," you lose. Your inner voice is taking you down with each variation of "I can't." Put "delete negative self-talk" at the top of your to-do list.

Procrastination: Putting off something and rationalizing that it's the wrong time or that you're not ready usually means you are afraid to fail. Fear of failing is guaranteed to be a major roadblock to your success.

Anyone who is a procrastinator is also quite good at negative self-talk. Procrastination is a form of suicide, just in slow motion. If you are a procrastinator, your speech is probably littered with phrases such as, "If only..." or "I can't afford to" or "I'll get around to it one of these days" or "I don't have the time", etc.

Procrastination occurs for a variety of reasons. Leading the list is the feeling, *I don't want to succeed.* There is an actual fear of success and of the possible failure that could be part of it. If you put it off until tomorrow, someone else may come in and do the project.

Or, if it doesn't work when someone else does it, you can rationalize and say it was a mistake or shouldn't have been done in the first place. Anyone who procrastinates avoids doing things that they perceive as discomfitting or simply overwhelming.

Many women procrastinate when making decisions about participating in projects, or even putting their resumes in for promotion consideration. It is common to see men jump into projects—any projects—even when they know very little about the tasks required. Their attitude is that they can figure it out along the way. Women are different—women want to know all the nuances, the pros and cons and how to do "it" before they will commit.

Women fear they may actually get it—the project or promotion—and if it doesn't work out or they don't work out, their problems are compounded. Then they will look foolish...or a failure in others' eyes. Men view it as their best shot—if it works, great, if it doesn't, the world doesn't end. By procrastinating, women practice the art of avoidance and enforce their fear of failure.

Misplaced Loyalty: Loyalty can be blinding. You love your job and you love your employer—you are loyal. Yet an employer professes love for the employees only when the bottom-line profit picture is satisfactory—the company is loyal, but its "love" is conditional. And so it also goes when you are working on projects within your community—if all is well, all is well for you.

Women are more likely to hang onto their present positions, even when job security is at an all-time low. They continue to believe "The boss needs me," "I'm the only one who knows where everything is," "I can't desert them when everyone else is leaving them," or "I love my job." All these emotional responses don't include a shred of the logic needed in today's volatile employment situations. Men decide that they want off the ship before it sinks.

Okay, so you feel emotionally attached to your job. Think rationally now. Does *it* really love you? Does *it* call you when you are blue and need an encouraging word? Does *it* bring you a cup of tea when you don't feel well? Does *it* share an intimate story with you? Does *it* make you laugh? Does *it* wipe your tears or give you a hug at just the right moment? Does *it* tell you that you are wonderful, even when you don't feel wonderful? Does *it* tell you that you look terrific, even when you have a "bad hair" day? The answer is No! Individuals at work may do those things, but the company itself is like the Tin Man from *The Wizard of Oz*: It has no heart. And, sadly, it isn't even looking for one.

When things sour in the workplace, it is easy to rationalize why someone adopts a "hands off" or "let it be" posture, choosing the status quo rather than seeking a new situation. The two primary reasons are fear and denial. That includes fear of change itself and fear of not being able to get another job. Denial means not believing change could have a negative impact. But if you stay loyal to your fickle company or a relationship and live with that fear and denial for a period of time, what happens to you as a person?

Outsmarting The SeXX Factor

As a rule, no behavior is changed overnight; it takes time. In fact, it takes lots of reminders and reinforcements that reactions or responses may not be okay or are inappropriate. It's also important to develop realistic expectations of those opposite sex or same sex people with whom you interact in your personal and work lives. They are not going to change overnight either, but it doesn't mean they can't change.

Removing the Sabotage Trap

When you engage in self-sabotage, it is like erecting a barbed wire enclosure around yourself. Moving on to other enterprises or personal pursuits is substantially inhibited. One of the first steps to removing the self-sabotage trap is to be aware of when you work against yourself. When Kristi Yamaguchi won the Gold Medal at the 1992 Winter Olympics, commentator and former gold Olympian Scott Hamilton remarked, "Kristi's strength is her lack of weakness." A decade later, she's no different.

By knowing what your weaknesses are and in what areas you engage in self-sabotage, you can initiate a concentrated effort to eliminate such destructive behaviors from your life. When you deny that you self-sabotage, whether the behavior is negative self-talk, procrastination or being too personal, you do yourself no favors. If it is a problem, you need to acknowledge it. Are you alone? Absolutely not—everyone has practiced the art of self-sabotage at some time.

Part of having more power, authority, prestige and money is becoming more rounded. We women don't have the luxury of having any sharp edges hanging out.

       – Alice,
       Financial Analyst

15

Winning With Men
At Work and In Life

You now know there is more to achieving success in your interactions with men than being brilliant, witty, organized and loyal. You may have cringed at some of the advice we gave you—watch the jewelry you wear, don't brag so much, give the guy space, quit acting so smart that you end up intimidating others. But as a woman determined to successfully handle interactions with men, you are finding that this is all about making conscious choices, not giving in—or giving up who you are.

The woman who wants to succeed doesn't necessarily need to change her behavior at work or in her private life. Rather, she will begin to change her attitude to help her manage the way she thinks about her relationships with men. She is beginning to understand that the SeXX Factor exists and she is learning how to moderate those actions that often trigger men's discomfort, anger and confusion.

Women must interact with men in their private lives, in their domains as wives, mothers and involved citizens. In order to do so successfully, they must deal with characteristics, traits and behavioral patterns which cause friction between the sexes.

In the work arena, women wanting power, prestige and financial reward know that men hold the power over who gets into that world. They also know that men have always done what it takes to get that power...to get to the top. Women who have successfully made it to the top also are doing what it takes. They understand and are managing the SeXX Factor...intuitively, intellectually and spiritually.

First, Get in There...
It's your choice. The way to successful interactions between men and women, whether in personal or professional spheres, is a result of your conscious attitude shift. The successful woman knows that first she must *enter* the male power culture. Once in that culture she can work to *become* a true part of the culture in subtle ways with strategic shifts of attitude. She will then be in a position to *change* the culture for herself and all other qualified women.

You know the statistics in the work world. Women are *not* gaining equal status with their male counterparts to positions of power. Women hold only 8 percent of the top CEO positions in the United States. While this small percentage may be perceived as an improvement over the past decade, statisticians predict that at the current rate of growth it will take women another *hundred years* to finally gain equal parity with men in the world of work!

Women received the right to vote in 1920. Over eighty years later they must still break through "glass ceilings," fight their way toward top positions and demand that legislative action give them an equal chance. Many women agree on one thing: In order to gain equal status in positions of power, they must first enter the male culture.

Some women believe they can change the existing culture from the outside. They eventually can...but it will take them too long. Women must find another way to enter that male culture—sneak in if they can, sight unseen.

Says Cynthia, a successful CEO in a financial institution:

> *Successful career women know that they can get to the top in one of two ways: the long way or the easy way. The long way says take me as I am... I'll get there in spite of men, in spite of any obstacles.*

The wise woman knows that time is limited. She has seen how long it has taken for women to occupy those few top CEO positions open to them. She intuitively has known about the SeXX Factor all along, but couldn't put her finger on it. This woman knows that she must play the game in order to gain passage into a man's world.

...Then Become the Culture
Once women enter the male culture they can begin to do everything they can to learn how it works. They shall "become the culture," so to speak. They shall work with the key players (men) and discover why

men (and women) continue to promote men to positions of power. They will become familiar with the male culture and begin to change that culture.

For example, women who finally gain access to CEO positions have known all along that they have had to manage their actions in order to get to the top. Once there, they can assimilate that behavior into the male culture and prove that they belong there. They will continue to manage the SeXX Factor and its effect on men at work. They will continue to moderate their speech, levels of femininity, urge to control male subordinates, etc. and work to "bring" more women into top positions through mentoring and informal networking, and finally, through promotions. Women will be able to fill the pipeline to top positions with other women who know how to handle the SeXX Factor.

...and Finally, Change the Culture

When women have established their ground as powerful leaders and managers and have moved into an equitable number of top CEO positions in the United States, they will be able to change how things work for all women. Women at the top and those wanting access to positions of power will finally be able to say, "I like myself, I'm not changing... I'm not changing my speech, my dress, my hair, my leadership style for anyone. This position is mine!"

You're Not Done Yet

Today, the SeXX Factor is still a major roadblock that limits women's advancement in their careers and personal lives. While not all ambitious men succeed, the majority of individuals promoted in any organization continues to be men. Women wanting to succeed in their careers are familiar with the system, are prepared for competition and understand and accept that sex role differences will be difficult to overcome. These women continue to capitalize on their strengths, recognize their weaknesses and work actively to improve upon them. They have learned to continuously outsmart the SeXX Factor.

It is critical for women who challenge traditional gender expectations to be aware of the ways in which the SeXX Factor can impact their relationships with both men and other women at work. Let's hear from the horses' mouths—

Harold, a chief executive, spoke about the importance of mentors:

A real big help for women would be to have mentors, not only women mentors, but also men mentors...people you could have a conversation with about things like the SeXX Factor. There are plenty of men around who want to see women in roles of leadership and authority.

Another top executive, Franklin, suggested that women must continue to push the limits:

This is an interesting time, because it's almost a role reversal. Bring yourself to the table, bring your skills to the table and be more magnanimous than males have been historically.

Samuel confirmed that women must find their own balance when they communicate with men:

Women are going to have to communicate in ways that are non-threatening to men but are still straightforward without falling back into the masculine type of behaviors, because that, in itself, impedes women's progress.

And....

People want to be with confident women in positions of authority who are not threatened by others. They don't have to raise their voices. They don't have to order people around. They don't have to remind people of the title they hold. People like that.

Stephanie, a female executive, spoke about the importance of the mix between intelligence and emotionality in the workplace:

Everyone is in agreement in wanting to see a person in authority have heart. But if you are all heart and you are not demonstrating the intellectual ability to make tough decisions, then the people who decide whether you get into the pool for advancement tend to be nervous about you.

Alice summed up her perceptions about women's tendency to demonstrate excessiveness:

*My advice to the emerging woman is **don't be too anything**. Don't be too sweet, don't be too caring. It's a matter of self-awareness and monitoring, because these are the characteristics that become exaggerated and therefore become eccentric, irritating and odd.*

These behaviors hurt a woman. Don't process too much, don't talk too much... The female needs to learn how to monitor her environment and figure out her appropriate place on the continuum. How much information she needs, how much closure she needs, how enthusiastic she should be. Find your normal range and stay there. That calls for some truncating of your normal, natural behaviors, but that's part of the deal.

Part of having more power, authority, prestige and money is becoming more rounded. We women don't have the luxury of having any sharp edges hanging out.

Win with Men Anywhere...Use the Same Rules

The good news is that getting it right will just about guarantee that all your relationships with men will benefit. The rules don't change—it's the same on the tennis court, at the auto mechanic shop, at your financial advisor's office, at your child's school or sport activities and in the physician's examination room—when women deal with the opposite sex.

Outsmarting The SeXX Factor

Successful Women . . .
- Control their urge to gain sexual power over men.
- Moderate their female advantage over men.
- Find their natural level of gender identity and stay there.
- Show compassion to men who have difficulty accepting and relating to powerful women.
- Express themselves in clear, direct and deliberate ways.
- Lead with skills that are purposeful and intentional.
- Compete with themselves rather than with men.

Success is often achieved by those who don't know that failure is inevitable.

– Coco Chanel

————————————16

Successful Women Know—And Do

Throughout our research and writing of *The SeXX Factor*, we've compiled an extensive list of characteristics of winning women. Here is our "short list" of what successful women know.

Successful women know how to manage men's fears of sexual harassment accusations and know that this issue makes men feel very uncomfortable. They make men feel at ease by having discussions about this extremely sensitive subject.

Successful women know that gossip about their associates, fellow committee members and other male figures in their work or family domains is detrimental to smooth interactions.

Successful women know that the "cutesy" stuff at work, in organizations or in their private lives doesn't cut it. They behave like women in positions of power, assuming a demeanor characterized by dignity.

Successful women know that sexual jokes, innuendoes and sensual talk and gestures will get them tickets, dates and short-term promotions, but not the respect they need for real success.

Successful women know that men are often fragile, especially when it comes to taking orders and suggestions or accepting improvement strategies from women. They know how to handle men with *care*.

Successful women know that men like to win and do not take kindly to being outdone by a female in public.

Successful women know that if they act too assertive, men will think that they are pushy...so they do it subtly.

Successful women know that if they wear an overly feminine or revealing outfit to work, to their children's school or to an organizational meeting, men may want to flirt with them, but will not treat them seriously or take orders from them.

Successful women know that they cannot cry in front of their associates when facing problems and failures. They know that men and women alike will think that they are too weak for any position of power.

Successful women know that they can't use words like *feels like, I sense* or *love ya.*

Successful women know that they may use profanity only in the privacy of their own homes, if at all—the work place or other public meeting places are not appropriate venues.

Successful women know that it might be a good idea to sometimes allow men to open doors for them or pull out chairs. It's not a big deal.

Successful women know that they should use their leadership skills with precision and deliberation. They know that collaboration with men must be done with advanced notice and a sense of purpose.

Successful women know that sharing power is the key to acquiring an effective style of leadership. They also know that men are unfamiliar with this style and that if they share too much of their power, it could eventually turn against them.

Successful women know that they are better off than most men at planning and that others are beginning to recognize this, too. They also know that men who aren't good at planning are beginning to look bad to others in comparison. They never make a big deal about this in public.

Successful women know that they are good at using intuitive skills to get people to do things for them. They also know how to refine this skill to an act of subtlety.

Successful women know that they are outdoing men in many skill areas and always give a heads up to their male counterparts.

Successful women know not to brag about their accomplishments. Instead they have learned and honed the subtleties of self-promotion.

Successful women know that their communication styles have caused men to experience numerous problems. They moderate their tendency to overabundant speech, make directive statements and never ever say, "I'm sorry..."

Successful women know that they would love to make friends by telling others what they have just heard about so and so...but they also know that if men found out that they had carried this rumor forward or started the rumor that THEY would *never* be trusted in the future.

Successful women know that if they want the window open because they're hot, they need to walk over to the window and open it.

Successful women know that they must solicit the opinions of others before they make a decision, because that's the best way to make one. They also know that men need to know why they're asking them for their opinion.

Successful women know that things have changed in work, family and home environments and that many men find this uncomfortable... They do not take advantage of this.

Successful women know that they will not talk about the meeting they attended the night before with over one thousand powerful women in attendance.

Successful women know that they got this position in an organization or workplace over the last guy and never mention another word about it to anyone.

Successful women know that some men may think that they got their jobs because they are "women." They do everything they can to help these men get over and through it.

Successful women know that they must not overdo everything or be too grandiose or bring two thousand party favors to the next meeting.

Successful women know that when they disagree with men, they try to do it with good sportsmanship.

Successful women know they are smart, but realize if they flaunt their intelligence, it could eventually destroy them.

Successful women know that some men still hate woman who have earned top positions and are aware that these same men may have the power to promote them. They also know not to bring this up, if at all possible...

Successful women know that they still need to work long hours, but also know that some men who have the "nine to five" mentality feel inferior when compared to them. Successful women have learned to moderate their urge to work till midnight.

Successful women know that male subordinates loathe being male subordinates; so the women always make subordinate men feel like "powerful" men.

Successful women know that men who experience the SeXX Factor want it to go away.

You may have more scenarios to add to our list. Our bottom line is to bring up your consciousness level as to what works and what doesn't work when men and women need to interact. In the next chapter, we will sum up our theory and create an action plan for changing power static between the sexes into smooth interchanges. It is a plan you can implement, beginning today.

You miss 100 percent of the shots you don't take.

– Wayne Gretzky

17

Putting it All Together: Creating a Plan That Works

The areas we've addressed throughout *The SeXX Factor* and recommendations we've made via the **Outsmarting The SeXX Factor** tips are designed to help you interact successfully with men in your work, personal, social, family and home lives. The information given and ideas and tips suggested are based on years of experience investigating women's issues, combined with the latest research—some of it our own, some of it based on that of others. Let's revisit its definition:

The SeXX Factor

Behaviors, attitudes and strategies of women that inhibit, encumber or impede them in their private, family and work lives. These behaviors produce a subconscious discomfort or uneasiness in men, who react by getting angry, confused or resentful. Women end up dealing with unnecessary roadblocks and traps in both their personal and professional domains.

The basic tenets of learning to deal with the effects of the SeXX Factor are easy to understand and even easier to follow. The

Outsmarting The SeXX Factor tips throughout the book were gleaned from thousands of interviews about their personal and professional domains with men and women in positions of power in associations, charitable organizations, schools and universities, public and private corporations, small and large businesses and places where women and men gather, including churches, synagogues, association meetings and conferences, even brainstorming with groups of friends.

Both of us strongly believe in the saying, *Knowledge equals power.* But, and it is a large but, *knowledge* can do little unless it is *implemented.* The true equation is:

Knowledge + Implementation = Power

It's quite easy to talk, grumble and complain about roadblocks encountered. That's part of the knowledge quotient—to be able to do so and *focus* on the issues; it's also common to feel that you've got power because you can pinpoint and *reflect* on what the causes are and come up with some solutions; but none of the focusing or reflecting will generate much unless you *act.* Your new tasks now are to *Focus,* to *Reflect* and to *Act.*

The Focus = Knowledge

Start by reassessing your performance on *The SeXX Factor Quiz* in chapter 1. By now, you should better understand the impact of your behaviors on your private life and work environment, especially those that may trigger men (and sometimes other women) to experience the effects of the SeXX Factor. Throughout the book the behaviors were identified and explained. Take time to go back to the chapters relevant to your life and experiences and review them.

By developing your own awareness in areas you create that are contributory agents of the SeXX Factor, you will strengthen your resilience to offset the damaging effects on your career and your access to everyday power.

Select three to five target behaviors that you personally believe you can work on to change so that you can improve the way you relate to the men in your life. Use the following table to focus your target behaviors:

Target Behaviors

Five focus areas or behaviors that I intend to target include:

1. _____

2. _____

3. _____

4. _____

5. _____

The Reflection = Implementation

To get the most from the concepts we have discussed, you not only need to reflect on the workings of your own personality and behavior styles, but you also need to consult with critical friends to verify that the changes you make in your work style are having the desired effects.

We encourage you to start building your personal library—books, videos, CDs and DVDs that focus on the areas that you have identified as ones you need to improve. Look for programs, seminars and workshops that are offered where you live and/or work that will enhance your communication and leadership skills.

If you belong to a professional group, it's common to have a "personal development" track at a conference or convention that you attend. Although those workshops are often considered "soft skills" compared to the programs offered that are clinical, technical or industry specific—"hard skills"—we contend that it's the soft skills and the lack of mastering them that continually set women back. Both of us are believers in mastery, which you can achieve through continuously using and improving skills, reflecting on goals and taking action.

We believe that it is possible to transform today's women into a powerful entity if groups of people are willing to take on the challenge of battling the effects of *The SeXX Factor* at work and in everyday life. What we need are people who can help change the male-dominated professions and a grassroots movement ensuring that the truth about male dissonance—any type of dissonance—in work and personal domains, instead of gender-specific politics, gets out to everyone.

The most convincing argument in achieving the goals of this book will be women and men having successful interactions and communications in all aspects of their lives.

Let your voice be heard—it's the way to create the necessary changes in our society. Visit our interactive Internet website at *www.seXXfactor.com*. Post your experiences, successes and comments on the message board; women everywhere can learn from each other in this global chat room!

In the meantime, find a critical friend and persuade her or him to join you in a women's group (one created by you). Initiate discussions with your group to reflect on the conscious choices that you have made to change your behaviors to better suit the work place. *A warning needs to be added.* Remember which behaviors bug men and create trigger points for them. Your ongoing gathering is not the place to let any of them surface. Your collaborative efforts will ultimately help you change your attitude, making long-term changes for all women.

Action = Power

Create a long-term action plan, launching your journey to positions of power. Use the simple charts that follow to facilitate this process. Display the chart in your planner or whatever you use to jog your memory—it's a new "To Do" list that is really a "To Act" list. Use it as an ongoing reminder of where you want to be and what you need to accomplish in order to achieve your goals.

Following are three different Action Plans. The first is a sample for a woman trying to achieve change in her personal activities. The second is a sample action plan for a work-related goal. The third is a blank for you to duplicate and use as you start your own journey toward successful interactions with men in your personal and professional life.

Action Plan 1 / Personal Domain

Goal: To become the next President of the Parent/Teacher Association.

Desired outcome dates	Essential Strategies	Accountability or Benchmarks
2/2003	1. End gossiping about other members	Start a diary of incidents and rumors to check on
2/2003	2. Do not publicly berate male board members	Have an associate give feedback on my success
3/2003	3. Offer concrete plans	Begin writing a plan for a new project
1/2003	4. Choose clothing in keeping with activities	Ask a friend to critique my choices

Action Plan 2 / Business Domain

Goal: To become the next Manager of the accounting department

Desired outcome dates	Essential Strategies	References/Benchmarks
1/2003	1. Limit the amount of my over talking	Ask a friend to spot check me on this
1/2003	2. Stop swearing in public	Keep a journal and record the number of times I slip up
2/2003	3. Allow men to open the door for me or help lift heavy packages, etc.	Record the number of times I allow this to happen
2/2003	4. Begin working from 8:00am to 4:30pm like everyone else	Log my daily hours in my planner

My Action Plan

Goal:

Desired outcome dates	Essential Strategies	Accountability or Benchmarks

Wake-Up Call to the Conscious

The word prejudice is very powerful and is directly linked to male dissonance—the SeXX Factor. For women who want to excel, it can create fear...and a dose of reality. If gender dissonance is in play, it's tough to be successful in one's interactions with the opposite sex. Period. When one's consciousness rises to understand what power static does, who is the recipient of it and who generates it—the road to correction and elimination is activated.

In dealing with any type of dissonance, it's important to become consciously aware of actions created from attitudes of prejudice (including your own). Until that happens, little can be done to change attitudes and actions that block women.

This book is filled with different scenarios for successful interaction with male associates, board members, subordinates and superiors at work. At times you will not be able to imagine doing or experiencing what is written. The achievement of your success is not to be construed as a "one-size-fits-all" concept, although there will be times when it will be a "one-size-fits-most" and times when it will be a "one-size-fits-few."

Rather, redefining successful interactions with men in your private and professional lives will be about having the freedom and courage to decide how far you want to go to achieve your power. As you figure out which strategies make up your own action plan, tap into the resources we've included in this book for inspiration, guidance, and ongoing personal reflection. Also, bear in mind, that sometimes it takes several tries before you can find the right answer. Along the journey, you will likely learn a great deal by trial and error.

Remember, your new awareness of the SeXX Factor may not be just about changing your own behavior. It may also be about changing the attitude generated from another person and monitoring the amount of dissonance created in your personal and career arenas.

Good luck on your journey to success, fulfillment and power. Having outsmarted the SeXX Factor, we believe you now have the tools to end gender dissonance and enjoy equal access in all areas of your life, from PTA meetings to executive boardrooms, from charity events to interacting with your kids' basketball coach.

References

We strongly believe that creating your own personal reference library (and reading and using the information) is one of the key factors in creating personal empowerment. Below are several of the books from our personal libraries. Some have been read many times, others just once. Many are plastered with Post-its®, slips of paper and other reminders of key sections that we routinely revisit.

Briles, J. *The Confidence Factor.* Aurora CO: Mile High Press, 2002.
_____. *Woman to Woman 2000.* Far Hills, NJ: New Horizon Press, 1999.
Buckingham, M. and Coffman, C. *First, Break All the Rules.* New York: Simon & Schuster, 1999.
Carnegie, D. *How to Win Friends and Influence People.* New York: Pocket Books, 1936, revised 1972.
Chesler, P. *Woman's Inhumanity to Woman.* New York: Nation Books, 2001.
Dowling, C. *Perfect Women.* New York: Summit Books, 1988.
Duck, J. *The Change Monster.* New York: Crown Business, 2001.
Eichenbaum, L. and Orbach, S. *Between Women.* New York: Viking Penguin, 1988.
Evans, G. *Play Like a Man, Win Like a Woman.* New York: Broadway, 2000.

Freidan, B. *The Feminine Mystique.* New York: W.W. Norton & Co., 1983.

Gallagher, C. *Going to the Top.* New York: Viking, 2000.

Gaylin, W. *The Male Ego.* New York: Viking Press, 1992.

Germer, F. *Hard Won Wisdom.* New York: Perigee, 2001.

Gilberd, P. *The Eleven Commandments of Wildly Successful Women.* New York: Macmillan Spectrum, 1996.

Glass, L. *Toxic People.* New York: St. Martin's Press, 1997.

Gray, J. *Men Are from Mars, Women Are from Venus.* New York: HarperCollins, 1992.

Grymes, S. and Stanton, M. *Coping with the Male Ego in the Workplace.* Stamford, Connecticut: Longmeadow Press, 1993.

Farrell, W. *The Myth of Male Power.* New York: Simon & Schuster, 1993.

Foley, M. *Bodacious!* New York: Amacon, 2001.

Hagberg, J. Real Power. Salem, Wisconsin: Sheffield Publishing Company, 2002.

Harragan, B.L. *Games Mothers Never Taught You.* New York: Rawson Associates, 1977.

Heim, P. and Murphy, S. *In the Company of Women.* New York: Tarcher Putnam, 2001.

Helgesen, S. *The Female Advantage: Women's Ways of Leadership.* New York: Doubleday, 1990.

Hyatt, C. *Shifting Gears.* New York: Simon & Schuster, 1990.

Hyatt, C., and Gottlieb, L. *When Smart People Fail.* New York: Simon & Schuster, 1993.

Jeffers, S. *Feel the Fear and Do It Anyway.* New York: Random House, 1988.

Leonard, G. *Mastery.* New York: Dutton, 1991.

Lerner, H.G. *The Dance of Anger.* New York: HarperCollins, 1990.

_____. *The Dance of Deception.* New York: HarperCollins, 1993.

Levant, R. *Masculinity Reconstructed: Changing the Rules of Manhood— At Work, in Relationships, and in Family Life.* New York: Dutton, 1995.

Miller, J.B. *Toward A New Psychology of Women.* Boston: Beacon Press, 1976.

Pease, B.A. *Why Men Don't Listen and Women Can't Read Maps.* New York: Welcome Rain Publishers, 2000.

RoAne, S. *How to Work A Room.* New York: Quill, 2000.

Rosener, J. *America's Competitive Secret: Utilizing Women as a Management Strategy.* New York: Oxford University Press, 1995.

Sanford, L.T and Donovan, M. E. *Women and Self-Esteem.* New York: Viking Penguin, 1984.

Schaef, A.W. *Women's Reality.* Minneapolis: Winston Press, 1985.

Schapiro, N. *Negotiating for Your Life.* New York: Henry Holt & Company, 1993.

Sheehy, G. *New Passages.* New York: Random House, 1995.

Swiss, D.J. *The Male Mind at Work: A Woman's Guide to Working with Men.* Cambridge, Massachusetts: Perseus Publishing, 2000.

Tannen, D. *That's Not What I Meant.* New York: Ballantine Books, 1992.

_____. *You Just Don't Understand.* New York: Quill, 2001.

_____. *Talking from 9 to 5.* New York: Quill, 2001.

_____. *The Argument Culture.* New York: Ballantine Books, 1999.

Tavris, C. *The Mismeasure of Women.* New York: Simon & Schuster, 1992.

Wilson, L. and Wilson, H. *Play to Win.* Austin, Texas: Bard Press, 1998.